1

This book belongs to:

_____

Aquarius Daily Horoscope 2025

Author's Note: Time set to Coordinated Universal Time Zone (UT±0)

Contents

The 12 Zodiac Star Signs

2025

January

S	M	T	W	T	F	S
			1	2	3	4
5	6	7	8	9	10	11
12	13	14	15	16	17	18
19	20	21	22	23	24	25
26	27	28	29	30	31	

February

S	M	T	W	T	F	S
						1
2	3	4	5	6	7	8
9	10	11	12	13	14	15
16	17	18	19	20	21	22
23	24	25	26	27	28	

March

S	M	T	W	T	F	S
						1
2	3	4	5	6	7	8
9	10	11	12	13	14	15
16	17	18	19	20	21	22
23	24	25	26	27	28	29
30	31					

April

S	M	T	W	T	F	S
		1	2	3	4	5
6	7	8	9	10	11	12
13	14	15	16	17	18	19
20	21	22	23	24	25	26
27	28	29	30			

May

S	M	T	W	T	F	S
				1	2	3
4	5	6	7	8	9	10
11	12	13	14	15	16	17
18	19	20	21	22	23	24
25	26	27	28	29	30	31

June

S	M	T	W	T	F	S
1	2	3	4	5	6	7
8	9	10	11	12	13	14
15	16	17	18	19	20	21
22	23	24	25	26	27	28
29	30					

July

S	M	T	W	T	F	S
		1	2	3	4	5
6	7	8	9	10	11	12
13	14	15	16	17	18	19
20	21	22	23	24	25	26
27	28	29	30	31		

August

S	M	T	W	T	F	S
					1	2
3	4	5	6	7	8	9
10	11	12	13	14	15	16
17	18	19	20	21	22	23
24	25	26	27	28	29	30
31						

September

S	M	T	W	T	F	S
	1	2	3	4	5	6
7	8	9	10	11	12	13
14	15	16	17	18	19	20
21	22	23	24	25	26	27
28	29	30				

October

S	M	T	W	T	F	S
			1	2	3	4
5	6	7	8	9	10	11
12	13	14	15	16	17	18
19	20	21	22	23	24	25
26	27	28	29	30	31	

November

S	M	T	W	T	F	S
						1
2	3	4	5	6	7	8
9	10	11	12	13	14	15
16	17	18	19	20	21	22
23	24	25	26	27	28	29
30						

December

S	M	T	W	T	F	S
	1	2	3	4	5	6
7	8	9	10	11	12	13
14	15	16	17	18	19	20
21	22	23	24	25	26	27
28	29	30	31			

2025

Daily Horoscope

AQUARIUS

As your astrologer, I wish to explain why one horoscope book may differ from another for each zodiac sign. The vast array of astrological activity constantly occurring in the sky requires me to focus on the essential aspect of the star sign I am writing for on any given day. Each zodiac sign is unique, and the various planetary factors affect them differently.

When crafting horoscopes, I pay special attention to the significant astrological aspects directly impacting a specific sign. By doing so, I can provide the most insightful and relevant guidance to individuals of that zodiac sign. While there might be multiple planetary alignments on a particular day, one aspect may hold more significance for a specific sign than others.

Considering the ruling planets and elements associated with each zodiac sign further refines my interpretations. This attention to detail ensures that the horoscope resonates with the distinct characteristics and tendencies of the star sign in question.

Ultimately, I aim to offer personalized insights and advice based on each zodiac sign's unique cosmic influences. By focusing on each star sign's most relevant astrological aspects, I can help readers better understand themselves and navigate the energies surrounding them. Embracing each zodiac sign's strengths, challenges, and opportunities allows me to create a horoscope book tailored to my readers' needs.

"We are born at a given moment, in a given place, and, like vintage years of wine, we have the qualities of the year and the season of which we are born. Astrology does not lay claim to anything more."

—Carl Jung

JANUARY

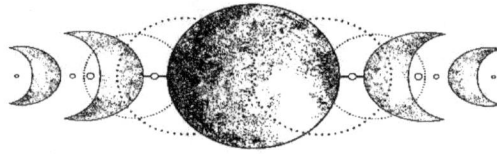

MOON MAGIC

Sun	Mon	Tue	Wed	Thu	Fri	Sat
			1	2	3	4
5	6	7	8	9	10	11
12	13	14	15	16	17	18
19	20	21	22	23	24	25
26	27	28	29	30	31	

NEW MOON

WOLF MOON

30 Monday

With the Moon ingress Capricorn and the arrival of the New Moon, you may feel a strong sense of determination and a desire to establish solid foundations in various aspects of your life. The energy of Capricorn encourages discipline, responsibility, and a diligent work ethic. It's a favorable period for taking on new responsibilities, organizing priorities, and making long-term plans. Embrace the transformative energy of this New Moon to lay the groundwork for success.

31 Tuesday

New Year's Eve brings a sense of anticipation and excitement as you reflect on the year that has passed and look forward to the year ahead. It's a time for celebration, whether you ring in the new year with friends and family or by yourself. You feel a sense of renewal and the opportunity for a fresh start as you contemplate your goals and aspirations for the coming year. It's a time to set intentions and make resolutions about your health, career, and relationships.

1 Wednesday

With the Moon entering Aquarius, a sense of innovation and individuality permeates the air. The energy of this transit encourages you to connect with individuals who share your values. It's an ideal time to set intentions for the year that align with your authentic self and contribute to the greater good. Embrace your eccentricities and let your originality shine as you embark on a fresh start, guided by the forward-thinking and progressive energy of the Aquarius Moon.

2 Thursday

Under the cosmic gaze, your home takes center stage, inviting a theme of improvement and transformation. Consider this celestial encouragement as an opportunity to make positive changes within your living space. Whether it's decluttering to create a serene environment, redecorating to infuse new energy, or organizing to enhance functionality, each action contributes to the creation of a more harmonious and pleasant home sanctuary.

3 Friday

With Mars opposing Pluto, you may encounter intense power struggles and conflicts that test your resilience. It's essential to approach these challenges with assertiveness and integrity, avoiding manipulative tactics. This alignment requires confronting and transforming destructive patterns or habits hindering your growth. As the Moon enters Pisces, your emotions amplify, and you may find solace in creative pursuits, introspection, and connecting with your spiritual side.

4 Saturday

During the Sun sextile Saturn aspect, you can establish a solid foundation for your goals and aspirations. This alignment brings a sense of discipline, responsibility, and perseverance to your endeavors. You are encouraged to take a structured and organized approach to achieve long-term success. This aspect supports you in taking on responsibilities and commitments with a sense of maturity and wisdom. Embrace the disciplined mindset and the opportunities that arise for growth.

5 Sunday

With the Moon entering Aries, you may experience a surge of energy and assertiveness. This lunar transit inspires you to take charge and initiate new beginnings in various areas of your life. Your emotions will likely be passionate and intense, fueling your drive to pursue your desires enthusiastically. It's a time to embrace your inner warrior and fearlessly go after what you want. Trust your instincts and be bold in expressing your authentic self.

6 Monday

A combination of Mars in Cancer and Mercury square Neptune invites you to balance your assertiveness with empathy and sensitivity. Find ways to express your emotions and assert yourself while also considering the feelings and perspectives of others. You can navigate these influences with grace and understanding by cultivating open and honest communication and staying grounded in reality.

7 Tuesday

With the Moon entering Taurus, you may experience a shift towards a more grounded and stable emotional state. Your focus turns to the practical aspects of life, emphasizing comfort, security, and physical pleasures. You may seek out and appreciate the simple pleasures in life, such as good food, physical touch, and a cozy environment. You will be more patient and steadfast in your emotions, seeking stability and reliability in your relationships and daily routines.

8 Wednesday

Mercury ingress Capricorn, you draw topics related to career, success, and achieving tangible results. It's an excellent time to set clear objectives, plan, and engage in goal-oriented discussions. Take advantage of this period to attend to important tasks, establish productive routines, and communicate your ideas with confidence and pragmatism. Your ability to think strategically and articulate effectively leads to successful outcomes and practical solutions.

9 Thursday

With the Sun illuminating your twelfth house, the Capricorn energy takes on a more reflective and private quality. Your disciplined and ambitious nature is turned inward, leading to a deep exploration of your subconscious and spiritual realms. You may find solace in solitude and contemplation, seeking to understand the hidden aspects of your psyche. Allow yourself the space for rest and rejuvenation to balance the demands of your ambitious pursuits.

10 Friday

With the Moon ingressing Gemini, you experience a shift in your emotional energy and a heightened sense of curiosity. Your mind becomes more active and adaptable, and you crave mental stimulation and variety. This transit encourages you to explore new ideas, engage in meaningful conversations, and seek diverse perspectives. You may find yourself more talkative and friendly, eager to connect with others and share your thoughts and experiences.

11 Saturday

As the celestial conductor orchestrates the cosmic symphony of your emotions, allow the stars to guide you through a harmonious exploration of your inner world. It is a time to attune yourself to the subtle melodies of your feelings, embracing the cosmic currents that lead you toward emotional resonance and balance. Listen closely to the celestial notes, and let the music of your soul guide you toward a deeper understanding of your emotional landscape.

12 Sunday

You may feel inspired to channel your energy into creative pursuits or spiritual practices. The harmonious alignment of Mars and Neptune fuels your imagination and allows you to manifest your dreams into reality. Trust your instincts and listen to your heart's desires during this time. Focus on creating a peaceful and nurturing atmosphere within yourself and your external surroundings. Connecting with your inner world brings you a sense of fulfillment.

13 Monday

Today is a good time to let go of what no longer serves you and embrace personal growth. Combining the Sun trine Uranus and the Full Moon creates an atmosphere of excitement, self-discovery, and empowerment. Embrace the energy of this period to embrace your true self, embrace change, and make positive shifts in your life. Trust your intuition, honor your emotions, and allow yourself to step into the fullness of your potential.

14 Tuesday

As the Moon enters Leo and Venus forms a square with Jupiter, you are stepping into a vibrant and expressive phase filled with opportunities for growth and expansion. The Moon's ingress into Leo brings a sense of confidence, creativity, and playfulness to your emotions, encouraging you to shine your light and express yourself with joy. Meanwhile, the square between Venus and Jupiter presents a dynamic tension between the desire for indulgence and the need for moderation.

15 Wednesday

In the sixth house, Mars in Cancer directs its assertive and energetic qualities towards your work and health routines. You approach your daily tasks with a nurturing and protective attitude, often going above and beyond to ensure the well-being of those around you. Your work ethic is fueled by emotional investment, and you may find fulfillment in roles that allow you to care for others or make a positive impact on the community.

16 Thursday

The Sun's opposition to Mars brings a clash between your desires and your sense of self-expression. There is a potential for conflicts and power struggles to arise, as you may feel a push-pull dynamic between asserting yourself and maintaining harmony. The ingress of the Moon into Virgo adds practical and detail-oriented energy to the mix. You may find yourself focused on organizing, problem-solving, and attending to the finer details of your life.

17 Friday

With the Sun sextile Neptune, you will likely experience a harmonious blend of inspiration and intuition. This aspect opens the door to a greater connection with your dreams, imagination, and spiritual realm. You may find yourself more attuned to subtle energies and have a heightened sensitivity to the needs and emotions of others. This transit is an excellent time to engage in creative pursuits, spiritual practices, and activities that nourish your soul.

18 Saturday

In the reflective twelfth house, Mercury in Capricorn indicates a deep and strategic mindset in matters of spirituality, hidden knowledge, and the subconscious. Your thoughts may be contemplative and disciplined, and you may find fulfillment in solitary pursuits such as meditation or reflective writing. Your communication style may be reserved, and you could excel in behind-the-scenes roles where your strategic thinking is applied to support broader spiritual or humanitarian goals.

19 Sunday

As the Sun moves into Aquarius, you may feel a renewed sense of individuality and a desire to express your unique self within the context of a larger community. This planetary alignment encourages you to embrace your authentic self and contribute your ideas and ideals to collective endeavors. It's a time for embracing your uniqueness while fostering camaraderie and collaboration with like-minded individuals. It is a valuable time for joint projects and collaborative initiatives.

20 Monday

Today's celestial alignment places a spotlight on the interconnected constellations of your social life. Reach out to friends, make plans to connect with loved ones, or venture into uncharted territories to expand your social circle. The cosmic encouragement emphasizes the profound impact of meaningful interactions, bringing not only joy but also a sense of belonging and community into the intricate tapestry of your life.

21 Tuesday

As the Moon ingresses Scorpio, it amplifies the intensity of your emotions and fosters a desire for emotional depth and authenticity. You may find yourself drawn to explore the mysteries of life and delve into profound emotional connections. It is a time for embracing the shadows, healing, and rebirth. You have the potential to tap into your inner strength and resilience, allowing you to overcome challenges and emerge stronger than before.

22 Wednesday

In the second house, Venus in Pisces influences your values and approach to material possessions, financial matters, and self-worth. You may have a soft spot for artistic or spiritual investments and find fulfillment in surrounding yourself with beauty. Financial decisions are influenced by your desire for comfort and a harmonious environment. Be mindful to strive for practicality while still appreciating the sentimental value of your possessions.

23 Thursday

With Mars sextile, Uranus brings dynamic and electric energy that fuels your drive for independence and innovation. This alignment brings enthusiasm and courage to embrace change and break from routine. You may draw unique and unconventional ideas and be eager to take bold and spontaneous actions. However, as Mercury opposes Mars, there's potential for disagreements, as your thoughts and words may clash with your assertiveness and desires.

24 Friday

With the Moon ingress Sagittarius, you may experience a shift in your emotional landscape. This aspect brings a sense of adventure and a desire for exploration and expansion. You may feel a renewed enthusiasm for life and a craving for new experiences. A need for freedom and a broader perspective may influence your emotions. Embrace the freedom and openness of this lunar transit, allowing yourself to enjoy the vast possibilities.

25 Saturday

Venus trines Mars. Your interactions with others are characterized by warmth and cooperation, making finding common ground easier and creating mutually beneficial outcomes. Your creative endeavors are supported, and you may take bold steps toward manifesting your artistic visions. Embrace this harmonious energy between Venus and Mars, and allow it to guide you toward fulfilling your desires with passion and grace.

26 Sunday

As Mercury sextiles Neptune, your thoughts and communication take on a dreamy and imaginative quality. Your intuition and creativity heighten, allowing you to express yourself gracefully and sensitively. This aspect supports deep and meaningful conversations and spiritual and artistic pursuits. You can tap into your intuition and receive valuable insights from the subtle realms. With Venus sextile Uranus, social interactions have a spontaneous and exciting flavor.

27 Monday

A strategic blueprint unfolds before you, mapping out the trajectory of your career under the guidance of optimistic cosmic energies. Embrace the learning time that awaits, deepening your knowledge and refining your skills. This growth-driven phase sets the stage for a bright future, and as you follow the cosmic map, feel the exhilaration of your career path aligning with the positive forces that dance across the celestial canvas.

28 Tuesday

With Mercury ingress Aquarius, your thinking and communication style take on a more innovative and unconventional tone. Your mind becomes open to fresh ideas and unique perspectives, allowing you to think outside the box and embrace alternative viewpoints. Intellectual discussions and stimulating conversations help expand your horizons. This transit encourages you to express your individuality and share your ideas with others in a progressive and forward-thinking manner.

29 Wednesday

Coupled with the New Moon, this Mercury-Pluto conjunction signifies a fresh start and a powerful time for transformation. It encourages you to let go of outdated thought patterns and beliefs, allowing space for new insights and revelations to emerge. This alignment is a time of introspection and self-discovery, where you can tap into your inner wisdom and make powerful changes in your thinking and communication style.

30 Thursday

With Uranus turning direct, you may experience a sense of liberation and forward momentum. This planetary shift brings energy and excitement, propelling you toward personal growth and breakthroughs. As Uranus awakens from its retrograde phase, you are encouraged to embrace your individuality and embrace change. It's a time to break free from old patterns and embrace new possibilities that align with your authentic self.

FEBRUARY

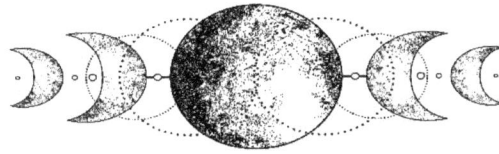

MOON MAGIC

Sun	Mon	Tue	Wed	Thu	Fri	Sat
						1
2	3	4	5	6	7	8
9	10	11	12	13	14	15
16	17	18	19	20	21	22
23	24	25	26	27	28	

New Moon

SNOW MOON

31 Friday

In the first house, your Aquarius Sun radiates a strong sense of individuality and a commitment to progress. A desire marks your personality for authenticity, uniqueness, and a forward-thinking approach to life. You often find fulfillment in expressing your original ideas and contributing to causes that promote innovation and social change. Be aware of a potential detachment from emotional expression and seek to balance your independent spirit with genuine connections with others.

1 Saturday

With Venus conjunct Neptune, you enter a dreamy and enchanting realm of love and beauty. This celestial alignment brings heightened sensitivity and compassion to your relationships and creative endeavors. You may yearn for deeper connections and seek experiences that touch your soul. Love takes on a mystical quality, inviting you to explore the depths of your emotions and embrace the power of unconditional love.

2 Sunday

Moon ingress Aries. The Aries Moon empowers you to assert your needs, set boundaries, and be true to yourself. Channel this dynamic energy into productive endeavors, and don't be afraid to step outside your comfort zone. Use this vibrant energy to initiate new projects, assert your boundaries, and take decisive steps toward your goals. Embrace the pioneering spirit of Aries and let your inner fire guide you towards exciting adventures and personal growth.

3 Monday

Mercury trine Jupiter encourages you to explore new horizons, expand your knowledge, and embark on intellectual adventures. It's a time of great potential and possibilities, where your curiosity and thirst for learning reward you. Embrace this alignment as a catalyst for personal and intellectual expansion, and let your ideas and insights inspire others. Trust your innate wisdom and allow curiosity to guide you toward new insights and discoveries.

4 Tuesday

With the Moon moving into Taurus, Venus entering Aries, and Jupiter turning direct, you are embarking on a period of growth, self-expression, and enhanced abundance. The grounding energy of the Taurus Moon brings stability and a deep sense of comfort to your emotions, allowing you to connect with your feelings and find pleasure in the simple joys of life. As Venus enters fiery Aries, you fill with passion, courage, and a renewed sense of self-worth.

5 Wednesday

As the cosmic clock ticks, directing the dance of celestial bodies, the focus shifts to the mastery of time management in the grand orchestration of daily life. Evaluate your daily routines and commitments with a discerning eye, seeking ways to enhance efficiency and productivity. The cosmic energies invite you to embrace effective time management practices, creating a symphony of balanced and fulfilling daily experiences.

6 Thursday

A curious and communicative energy sweeps in with the Moon transitioning into Gemini. You find yourself feeling mentally stimulated and open to new ideas and perspectives. This aspect is when your curiosity sparks, and you crave mental engagement and social interaction. Your mind becomes sharp, and your communication skills heighten, allowing you to express yourself easily and engage in stimulating conversations.

7 Friday

With Venus forming a harmonious sextile aspect to Pluto, a powerful and transformative energy permeates your relationships and personal connections. You draw experiences that deepen emotional intimacy and foster meaningful connections. This aspect invites you to explore the depths of your desires and embrace vulnerability in your relationships. You may be attracted to intense and passionate experiences, and your magnetic presence can draw others toward you.

8 Saturday

With the Moon moving into nurturing and sensitive Cancer, your emotions take center stage, and you may find yourself seeking comfort, security, and a sense of belonging. This lunar transit encourages connecting with your inner world and honoring your emotional needs. Moon ingress Cancer is a time to celebrate your feelings and prioritize self-care. Use this time to strengthen your bonds with family and loved ones, creating a supportive and loving foundation.

9 Sunday

As the Sun aligns with Mercury, your mind is sharp, and your communication skills heighten. This powerful conjunction brings clarity and focus to your thoughts and words, allowing you to express yourself with confidence and conviction. It's a good time for intellectual pursuits, problem-solving, and making important decisions. Your ability to articulate your ideas is enhanced, making it easier to convey your thoughts and connect with others effectively.

10 Monday

Moon ingress Leo is a time to embrace your unique gifts and talents and share them with the world. Allow your inner fire to ignite your enthusiasm and inspire others around you. By embracing the playful and passionate energy of the Leo Moon, you can truly bask in the spotlight and create a positive impact in your personal and social spheres. Allow the Moon in Leo to fuel your sense of self-worth and encourage you to take bold leaps forward.

11 Tuesday

When the Sun forms a square aspect with Uranus, you may experience a sense of restlessness and a desire for change and freedom. This aspect brings an electrifying energy that can disrupt the status quo and challenge established routines and structures. You may desire to break free from limitations and embrace your individuality. Unexpected events or sudden insights may shake things up and encourage you to step outside your comfort zone.

12 Wednesday

During a Full Moon, the Sun and the Moon are in opposition, illuminating the sky with their powerful energy. This phase marks a culmination and a heightened sense of awareness. It brings a time of reflection and introspection, where you can gain clarity and insight into various aspects of your life. The Full Moon's radiant light shines a spotlight on your emotions, allowing you to see things more clearly and bring forth what needs to be acknowledged and released.

13 Thursday

As the Moon moves into Virgo, you may feel a shift towards practicality, organization, and attention to detail. It is when you can find satisfaction in tending to the small tasks and responsibilities that contribute to your overall well-being. Your focus may turn towards efficiency and productivity as you seek to bring order to your daily routines and environments. Paying attention to the details can give you a sense of accomplishment and help you improve in various areas.

14 Friday

As Mercury moves into Pisces, you may embrace a more romantic and dreamy mindset. Your communication style becomes more intuitive and compassionate, allowing you to connect deeply with your loved ones. You can express your emotions and thoughts more sensitively, fostering understanding and empathy in your relationships. You can create memorable and meaningful experiences with your loved ones, making Valentine's Day a truly magical and heartfelt celebration.

15 Saturday

Moon ingress Libra is an excellent time to engage in conversations, negotiations, or collaborations, as you are more inclined to consider different perspectives and find a compromise. Your focus may shift towards creating a harmonious and aesthetically pleasing environment in your physical surroundings and relationships. Embrace the social energy of Libra and use it to foster connections, cultivate diplomacy, and create a sense of equilibrium in your life.

16 Sunday

The celestial homefront becomes a canvas for social connection and creative exploration. As you step into the comforting embrace of home, allow the stars to guide you in fostering an environment where friendship and creativity flourish. Whether it's a cozy gathering with loved ones or a home-based creative project, let the cosmic energy infuse your domestic space with warmth, laughter, and imaginative pursuits.

17 Monday

This opportune moment urges you to navigate the delicate interplay between you and those in your life. Open up channels of communication, allowing the free flow of emotions and fostering a deeper understanding. The celestial alignment acts as a gentle guide, encouraging harmonious interactions. It's an ideal period to address any lingering conflicts, offering a chance for resolution and the cultivation of more profound emotional bonds that stand the test of time.

18 Tuesday

As the Moon enters Scorpio, you may notice a deepening of emotions and a heightened sense of intuition. This transit invites you to explore the depths of your feelings and delve into your subconscious. You may find yourself drawn to introspection and reflective activities that allow you to uncover hidden truths and profound insights. Simultaneously, with the Sun entering Pisces, compassionate and imaginative energy envelops your being.

19 Wednesday

The cosmic energies encourage you to set audacious goals and craft a strategic plan that aligns with your deepest aspirations. Imagine yourself as a cosmic architect, designing the stepping stones to success, and let the stars illuminate the path ahead. Trust in the positive cosmic forces as they guide your career toward a luminous destination filled with success, fulfillment, and a celestial sense of optimism.

20 Thursday

Moon ingress Sagittarius. Mercury Square Jupiter. Sagittarius ignites your desire for exploration, both physically and intellectually. It encourages you to broaden your horizons, seek new experiences, and embrace a more optimistic outlook. With Mercury squaring Jupiter, there may be a tendency to indulge in excessive idealism or overconfidence in your beliefs. It's essential to balance your enthusiasm with practicality and critical thinking.

21 Friday

The celestial canvas paints strokes of inspiration, igniting a surge of creative energy in your life. Whether you're an artist, writer, or simply exploring a new hobby, embrace the cosmic sparks that fuel your imagination. This auspicious time beckons you to engage in creative endeavors, allowing your unique expressions to flourish. Unleash the artist within, explore uncharted creative territories, and let the joy of self-expression be your guiding light.

22 Saturday

As the Moon enters Capricorn, you begin a period of increased focus, ambition, and determination. Capricorn's energy encourages you to set practical goals, establish structure, and work diligently towards your objectives. You may take on responsibilities, organize your life, and prioritize your long-term plans. This lunar transit invites you to embrace discipline and perseverance as you align your emotions with your sense of purpose.

23 Sunday

With the Sun in Pisces gracing your second house, your values and approach to finances are infused with dreamy and intuitive energy. You may find that material possessions hold emotional significance for you, and a desire for spiritual fulfillment influences your financial decisions. Be cautious of tendencies towards escapism or economic impracticality, and strive to ground your ideals in practical reality while still honoring the spiritual dimensions of your material pursuits.

24 Monday

As Mars turns direct, you may feel a surge of energy and motivation that propels you forward in your endeavors. After introspection and reassessment, Mars' direct motion signals a time for action and assertiveness. You are now empowered to take decisive steps toward your goals and pursue your passions with renewed vigor. This celestial shift brings a sense of momentum, allowing you to overcome obstacles and push through any resistance.

25 Tuesday

As the Moon enters Aquarius, you may experience a shift in your emotional landscape, fostering a sense of intellectual curiosity and a desire for greater social connection. This ingress encourages you to embrace your uniqueness and explore innovative ideas. Simultaneously, the conjunction of Mercury and Saturn brings a focused and disciplined mindset to your thinking processes, offering structured and logical approaches as you seek clarity and practicality in decision-making.

26 Wednesday

Within the cosmic choreography, the spotlight now turns to the stage of your professional life. Embrace the opportunities for growth and advancement that the planets present. This favorable alignment encourages you to showcase your skills, take on new responsibilities, or explore avenues for professional development. Seize the cosmic momentum to propel your career journey forward with confidence and purpose.

27 Thursday

The sextile between Mercury and Uranus brings intellectual brilliance to your thoughts and communication. You are open to innovative ideas and sudden insights that can lead to exciting breakthroughs. This aspect supports thinking outside the box and embracing your unique perspective. It's a time to trust your instincts. You can uncover fresh perspectives by combining the intuitive energy of the Moon in Pisces with the mental agility of Mercury's sextile Uranus.

MARCH

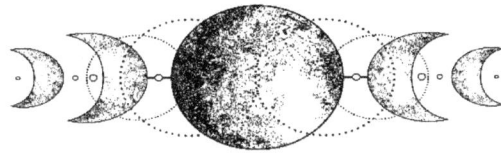

MOON MAGIC

Sun	Mon	Tue	Wed	Thu	Fri	Sat
						1
2	3	4	5	6	7	8
9	10	11	12	13	14	15
16	17	18	19	20	21	22
23	24	25	26	27	28	29
30	31					

New Moon

WORM MOON

28 Friday

The New Moon symbolizes a blank canvas where you can start anew and create your desired life. It is a powerful time to connect with your inner self, listen to your intuition, and make conscious choices that align with your most authentic desires. Embrace the energy of this cosmic reset and set your intentions with clarity and purpose. As the Moon begins its new cycle, you obtain a fresh start and the potential for transformation and growth in various areas of your life.

1 Saturday

You are infused with renewed vitality and enthusiasm, ready to pursue your passions with vigor. The Aries Moon empowers you to assert your needs and desires, encouraging you to embrace your inner warrior and boldly move forward. It's a time to embrace spontaneity, seize opportunities, and trust your ability to navigate the unknown. Allow this Aries energy to fuel your ambitions, inspire your actions, and ignite the fire within as you embark on a transformative journey.

2 Sunday

As Venus turns retrograde, it invites introspection and reflection on love, relationships, and personal values. You may revisit past experiences and reassess what truly matters to you in matters of the heart. Mercury, conjunct Neptune, allows for a deeper understanding of your emotions and the subtle nuances of communication. However, the Sun square Jupiter brings a potential clash between your aspirations and the need for realistic expectations.

MARCH

3 Monday

Mercury ingress Aries makes your thoughts and communication style more assertive and direct. You may feel a surge of enthusiasm and a desire to take quick action on your ideas and plans. Meanwhile, the Moon's ingress into Taurus brings a grounding and stabilizing energy to your emotions. You may find comfort and pleasure in simple pleasures, such as indulging in sensory experiences and cultivating a sense of security and stability.

4 Tuesday

As the planets align their wisdom, the cosmic forces beckon a focus on educational pursuits. Whether you are a dedicated student or an avid learner seeking new knowledge and skills, now is the ideal time to delve into the vast expanse of learning opportunities. Explore courses and workshops, or engage in self-directed study to broaden your intellectual horizons and embrace the cosmic gifts of enlightenment.

5 Wednesday

As the Moon enters Gemini, you may feel a curious mental agility. Your mind becomes sharp and receptive, ready to absorb new information and engage in stimulating conversations. This lunar transit encourages you to explore various perspectives and gather knowledge from different sources. Mercury sextile Pluto enhances your communication skills, allowing you to delve deep into meaningful discussions and uncover hidden insights.

6 Thursday

Change surrounds your world and soon brings the forwarding progress you have been seeking. It offers a chance to deepen a friendship as it shines a light on your personal goals. It fuels an exciting chapter of social engagement that leads to expanding horizons. It brings motivation, creativity, and growth to the forefront of your life. It opens a new page that lets you feel optimistic about prospects as it offers grounded foundations that nurture well-being and happiness.

7 Friday

As the Moon transitions into Cancer, you may experience a deep emotional sensitivity and nurturing energy. Your focus turns inward, and you find comfort in the familiar and the bonds of family and home. You may feel more connected to your emotions and intuition, seeking solace and security in your personal space. Your compassion and empathy heighten, allowing you better to understand the needs and feelings of those around you.

8 Saturday

With the harmonious alignment of the Sun and Mars in a trine aspect, you infuse with dynamic and confident energy. Your drive and assertiveness heighten, allowing you to take bold action and pursue your goals with passion and determination. This alignment brings a sense of vitality and enthusiasm to your endeavors, empowering you to step into leadership roles and assert yourself in various areas of your life.

9 Sunday

As the Moon moves into Leo, you feel a vibrant surge of energy and self-expression. Your emotions are bold and fiery, and you seek to shine. This lunar transit encourages you to embrace and share your creativity. You exude confidence and radiate warmth, drawing others towards your magnetic energy. It's a time to bask in the spotlight, embracing your unique qualities and expressing your authentic self.

MARCH

10 Monday

Feel the dynamic currents as Mars encourages you to approach your tasks with determination and emotional vigor. Under this celestial influence, your work environment becomes a battlefield where your emotional resilience and assertiveness shine. Mars invites you to infuse your daily routines with a passionate commitment to excellence, transforming challenges into opportunities for dynamic and professional growth.

11 Tuesday

When Mercury and Venus align, you reveal a harmonious blend of intellect and charm. Your communication style becomes more refined and persuasive, and you can naturally express your thoughts and emotions captivatingly. This alignment enhances your social interactions and fosters meaningful connections with others. You may engage in heartfelt conversations, sharing your ideas and desires quickly and gracefully.

12 Wednesday

When the Moon enters Virgo, and the Sun forms a conjunction with Saturn, you enter a period of practicality, discipline, and attention to detail. This alignment brings a focus on structure, responsibility, and long-term planning. You may feel a strong sense of determination and the need to establish a solid foundation for your goals and ambitions. The influence of Virgo encourages you to pay attention to the finer details and take a systematic approach to your tasks.

13 Thursday

With Mercury and Venus influencing your third house, your thoughts, communication, and relationships are marked by curiosity, social ease, and intellectual pursuits. You express yourself eloquently, and your communication style is often charming and diplomatic. Sibling relationships may play a significant role in your life, and you may find joy in creative writing, teaching, or engaging in intellectually stimulating activities.

14 Friday

With the Moon entering Libra, you seek harmony and compromise in your interactions. It is an excellent time to engage in cooperative efforts, mediate conflicts, and create a peaceful and supportive environment. By embracing the Full Moon energy, harnessing your individuality, and nurturing balanced relationships, you can experience growth, fulfillment, and a sense of harmonious connection.

15 Saturday

Mercury turns retrograde. Embrace the retrograde energy as a chance to gain deeper insights, reevaluate your strategies, and make necessary adjustments. Use this period to reconnect with yourself, listen to your intuition, and realign your actions with your true desires. Remember to be flexible and adaptable, as Mercury's retrograde motion invites you to embrace the unexpected and find creative solutions to any challenges.

16 Sunday

In the sanctuary of your home and family, Uranus in Taurus brings a cosmic whirlwind of innovation. Feel the revolutionary tremors as Uranus urges you to redefine your sense of security and domesticity. Under this celestial influence, your home becomes a laboratory for alternative ways of nurturing familial bonds. Uranus invites you to liberate yourself from outdated structures, fostering an atmosphere where individuality and freedom coexist with the comforts of home.

17 Monday

When the Moon ingresses into Scorpio, you may notice a deepening of emotions and a heightened sense of intensity. It is when you are likely to dive beneath the surface and explore the depths of your feelings. Your intuition and psychic abilities may heighten, allowing you to tap into hidden truths and uncover hidden motivations. It's a powerful time for personal transformation and introspection as you delve into the shadows and confront any unresolved issues.

18 Tuesday

Opportunity comes knocking soon. Any issues on the periphery of your life dissolve. You touch down in an abundant landscape that focuses on nurturing dreams. Being receptive to change is essential in growing your world. It lets you take advantage of expansive options overhead. It gets a chance to collaborate and nurture a venture that takes your talents to a broader audience. You reveal a pathway that draws growth and happiness.

19 Wednesday

As the Moon enters Sagittarius, a sense of adventure and optimism fills the air. It infuses your emotions with an understanding of adventure and expansiveness. You may feel a strong urge to explore new horizons externally and internally. This lunar phase encourages you to embrace a broader perspective, seek higher truths, and expand your understanding of the world. With the Sun conjunct Neptune, there is a touch of magic and enchantment around your life.

20 Thursday

As the Sun enters Aries, energy and enthusiasm ignite within you, marking the Vernal Equinox. It is a time of new beginnings, fresh starts, and the awakening of your inner fire. You feel renewed purpose and determination, ready to take on challenges and passionately pursue your goals. The Vernal Equinox represents a point of balance between day and night, symbolizing the equilibrium between light and darkness in your life.

21 Friday

Venus sextile Pluto. You are encouraged to embrace vulnerability, trust your instincts, and allow yourself to be fully present in matters of the heart. This alignment supports personal growth and the evolution of your relationships as you delve into intimacy, emotional healing, and empowerment. Open yourself to the transformative energy of Venus sextile Pluto, and embrace the profound shifts it can bring to your connections and sense of self.

22 Saturday

When the Moon ingresses Capricorn, you may experience a shift towards a more practical and disciplined mindset. Capricorn is an earth sign associated with ambition, responsibility, and a strong work ethic. During this time, you will likely focus on long-term goals, career aspirations, and building a solid foundation in various areas of your life. You may feel a heightened sense of determination and the need for structure and organization.

23 Sunday

Sun conjunct Venus. Sun sextile Pluto. Be open to the transformative energy that Pluto brings, as it encourages you to let go of what no longer serves you and embrace personal empowerment and growth. Through these alignments, you have the potential to experience profound shifts in your relationships and overall sense of self-worth. Trust in the transformative power of love and embrace the opportunities for growth and renewal that come your way.

24 Monday

When the Moon ingresses Aquarius, and the Sun forms a conjunction with Mercury, there is a harmonious fusion of intellectual brilliance and emotional detachment. Your thoughts and communication style align with your sense of individuality. You may express ideas unconventionally and embrace innovation. This alignment encourages you to think outside the box, question established norms, and seek intellectual stimulation that expands your horizons.

25 Tuesday

When Mercury sextiles Pluto, it brings a powerful blend of intellectual depth and transformative insights into your life. This aspect enhances your ability to delve into the depths of knowledge, uncover hidden truths, and engage in profound research or investigation. Your mind becomes sharper and more analytical, allowing you to perceive connections and patterns. This alignment also stimulates your communication skills, enabling you to convey ideas and opinions.

26 Wednesday

When the Moon enters Pisces, you may immerse in a dreamy and ethereal atmosphere. Your emotions become more fluid and intuitive, allowing you to tap into the subtle energies and unseen realms. This aspect is a time of heightened sensitivity and compassion, where you may feel deeply connected to the emotions and experiences of others. Your imagination soars, and you may draw artistic expression, music, or spiritual practices that nourish your soul.

27 Thursday

Trust in the power of your emotions and the transformative potential that lies within the depths of your being. Open yourself to the healing and transcendent energies present. Let the union of the Black Moon, Venus, and Neptune guide you on a profound journey of self-discovery and spiritual growth. Embrace the transformative power of this cosmic dance, and let it awaken your heart to the infinite possibilities of love and connection.

28 Friday

You may feel like asserting your independence, ready to tackle any challenges that come your way. The Aries Moon fuels your passion and drive, urging you to embrace your inner warrior and embrace new beginnings. Trust in your instincts and embrace the spirit of adventure as you navigate this dynamic and action-oriented energy. It's a time to embrace your individuality and fearlessly step into the world, ready to conquer whatever comes today.

29 Saturday

The New Moon is a time of new beginnings and possibilities, where the universe invites you to set intentions and plant seeds for the future. Take a moment to connect, tune into your heart's desires, and envision the life you seek. With each New Moon, you can align yourself with the natural cycles of the universe and embark on a journey of self-discovery and personal evolution. Embrace the fresh energy of the New Moon and allow it to manifest the highest potential.

30 Sunday

As Mercury enters Pisces and aligns with Neptune, your mind attunes to the depths of your imagination and intuition. This cosmic dance of Mercury and Neptune opens the gateway to heightened creativity, spiritual insights, and a profound connection to the unseen realms. With Neptune transitioning into Aries, you embark on self-discovery and self-expression as your dreams and visions become fiery and assertive.

APRIL

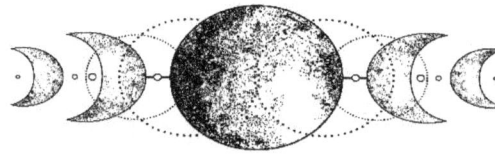

MOON MAGIC

Sun	Mon	Tue	Wed	Thu	Fri	Sat
		1	2	3	4	5
6	7	8	9	10	11	12
13	14	15	16	17	18	19
20	21	22	23	24	25	26
27	28	29	30			

NEW MOON

PINK MOON

31 Monday

In the realm of communication and intellectual pursuits, the Sun in Aries imparts a bold and expressive energy to your interactions. Conversations become dynamic, filled with passion and assertiveness. This cosmic alignment invites you to shine brightly in your exchanges with friends, fostering a courageous and adventurous approach to sharing ideas. The Sun in Aries encourages you to express your identity assertively through words and intellectual pursuits.

1 Tuesday

As the Moon enters Gemini, you feel a surge of mental energy and curiosity. Your mind becomes agile and adaptable, eager to explore new ideas and engage in lively conversations. This lunar transit encourages you to embrace the power of communication and intellectual stimulation. Your ability to express yourself with clarity and wit heightens, making it an ideal time for networking, learning, and sharing your thoughts with others.

2 Wednesday

There is a lot of potential surrounding your life; it brings the ideal moment to take the plunge and develop your dreams in a new area. A project you create begins to take shape, which connects you with more significant expansion that increases stability and security in your life. You move forward toward a remarkable trajectory of growth and advancement. Developing your abilities and nurturing your skills cracks the code to a robust phase of rising prospects.

3 Thursday

As the Moon moves into Cancer, you may feel a deep emotional connection and nurturing energy. Your focus turns towards your home, family, and inner world. This lunar transit invites you to embrace your sensitivity and intuition, allowing your emotions to guide you. You may find comfort in familiar surroundings and seek solace in the presence of loved ones. Your empathy and compassion heighten; you may naturally gravitate to a nurturing and calming environment.

4 Friday

As Saturn sextiles Uranus and Mars form a sextile with Uranus, you may experience a unique blend of stability and innovation. This harmonious alignment encourages you to balance tradition and progress, allowing you to embrace change while maintaining a solid foundation. You have the opportunity to tap into your creative and visionary side, finding new and exciting ways to approach challenges and pursue your goals.

5 Saturday

Mars trine Saturn is a time for taking decisive action, making steady progress, and building a solid foundation for endeavors. This planetary alignment empowers you to be strategic and purposeful in your industries. Embrace this harmonious energy and channel it into ambitions, knowing that the balanced alignment of Mars and Saturn supports your efforts. Trust in your abilities, stay focused on goals, and let this aspect empower you to reach new heights of achievement.

6 Sunday

With the Moon entering Leo, you reveal a vibrant and expressive energy. This lunar shift enhances your confidence, creativity, and desire for recognition. Combined with the Sun forming a harmonious sextile with Jupiter, you will likely experience a surge of optimism, enthusiasm, and a sense of expansion. This favorable alignment encourages you to embrace growth opportunities, take calculated risks, and believe in your abilities to succeed.

7 Monday

As Mercury turns direct, you can expect a shift in your communication and thought processes. Delays and misunderstandings during retrograde can clear up, allowing for smoother and more effective interactions. It's an excellent time to make decisions, initiate new plans, and move forward with greater clarity and confidence. Take advantage of this momentum to express yourself authentically, make essential choices, and engage in meaningful conversations.

8 Tuesday

With Venus forming a sextile aspect to Uranus, you may experience a delightful blend of harmony. It's an excellent time to prioritize self-care and establish healthy routines that support your well-being. Embrace the harmonious energy between Venus and Uranus to infuse your relationships and creative pursuits with excitement and individuality while leveraging the practicality of the Moon in Virgo to attend to the necessary details and structure your endeavors.

9 Wednesday

Events align to form a favorable window of opportunity. News arrives that lets you unpack new potential, ideas, and opportunities. It connects you with an edgy path that offers room to grow your abilities. Sharpening your skills and refining your talents shines a light on a progressive area that provides space to progress life forward. A fresh cycle beckons, bringing exciting developments that lead to a journey of growth and prosperity.

10 Thursday

You soon hit your stride in a new chapter of growth. Removing the heaviness and pushing back the barriers brings a lighter chapter that nurtures your abilities and grows your talents. You hit the road running and soon advance towards an inspiring time of increasing your skills and taking in new areas for development. It marks a bold beginning that transforms life as you build stable foundations that offer progression.

11 Friday

Moon ingress Libra. Your focus may shift towards creating peace and harmony in your environment, whether through cultivating harmonious relationships, beautifying your surroundings, or seeking out activities that bring stability and equilibrium. Libra's influence encourages you to find common ground, resolve conflicts, and cultivate peace. Embrace the gentle and harmonizing energy of the Moon in Libra to foster greater understanding and balance in your interactions.

12 Saturday

In the heart of your domestic sanctuary, Neptune casts its dreamy glow in the fourth house, infusing your home with an otherworldly ambiance. Feel the cosmic tides of emotional sensitivity and artistic expression as they gently permeate the walls of your abode. Under Neptune's celestial influence, create a haven of serenity where the energies of compassion and creativity blend seamlessly. Your home becomes a divine canvas, painted with the hues of intuition and empathy,

13 Sunday

Full Moon. Venus turns direct. Moon ingress Scorpio. This period calls for self-reflection, letting go of what no longer serves you, and embracing Scorpio's transformative energies. It's an opportunity to dive beneath the surface and uncover hidden truths within yourself and your connections with others. Allow the intense power of this time to guide you toward healing, growth, and a greater sense of authenticity.

14 Monday

An area you become interested in soon shows a great deal of promise. It transitions your focus to a chapter that offers room to see creativity blossom. It lays the foundations for improvement in your home circumstances. Unique opportunities crop up to encourage refining skills and using your inherent abilities. It rules a time of firing up creative skills and enjoying new areas that advance goals. It nurtures a strong foundation from which to grow your life.

15 Tuesday

Today brings fun, happiness, and joy into your surroundings. It lets you embrace the finer aspects of life. It brings a pleasing result that sees life improve in matters of social connection. It brings an enviable element that lights up new potential. Kicking away the cobwebs, you embark on an adventurous time of flying high with kindred spirits. It sets a positive trend that leaves you feeling rejuvenated and refreshed.

16 Wednesday

With the Moon's ingress into Sagittarius, you may feel a surge of enthusiasm and a thirst for adventure. Your emotions are infused with the fiery energy of Sagittarius, inspiring you to seek new experiences, expand your horizons, and embrace a sense of freedom. As Mercury also ingresses into Aries, your thoughts and communication style become more assertive and direct. You feel the urge to speak your truth and assert your ideas confidently.

17 Thursday

When Mercury aligns with Neptune in conjunction, it brings a dreamy and imaginative quality to your thoughts and communication. Your mind becomes attuned to the subtle realms of intuition, creativity, and spirituality. You may find yourself drawn to artistic pursuits, engaging in deep contemplation, or seeking a deeper understanding of life's mystical and metaphysical aspects. This alignment invites you to trust your instincts and listen to the whispers of your inner voice.

18 Friday

As Mars enters the fiery realm of Leo, your energy craves passion and self-expression. You feel a surge of confidence and desire to assert yourself boldly and creatively. Your actions feel guided by a strong sense of individuality and a willingness to take center stage. At the same time, the Moon's ingress into Capricorn adds a touch of practicality and a focus on long-term goals. You are motivated to work hard, set ambitious targets, and strive for success.

19 Saturday

Sun ingress Taurus. Mars trine Neptune alignment empowers you to pursue your dreams with inspired action and a compassionate approach. Trust your instincts and allow your imagination to guide you toward creative endeavors. With the energy of Taurus and the transformative influence of Mars trine Neptune, you can manifest your desires and bring your visions to life. Embrace this harmonious flow and let it guide you toward a fulfilling and purposeful journey.

20 Sunday

As Easter Sunday arrives, it brings with it a sense of renewal and rebirth. The vibrant energy of Venus sextile Uranus ignites a spark of excitement and a desire for freedom in your relationships and personal expression. You may feel drawn to explore new connections or embark on unconventional paths that bring unexpected joy and inspiration. At the same time, Mercury sextile Pluto's harmonious alignment empowers you to communicate your thoughts and ideas.

21 Monday

Sun square Mars aspect calls for a balance between assertiveness and patience as you navigate challenges and work towards your goals. By harnessing your inner strength and finding healthy outlets for your energy, you can transform this period of tension into an opportunity for growth and self-mastery. Remember to stay grounded and mindful of your interactions with others, seeking harmony and cooperation rather than engaging in unnecessary power struggles.

22 Tuesday

In the realm of creativity and self-expression, Jupiter in Gemini invites you to explore a vast array of artistic pursuits and intellectual adventures. Feel the expansive currents of inspiration as they surge through your creative endeavors, infusing them with a dynamic and versatile energy. Jupiter encourages you to turn the canvas of your self-expression into a cosmic masterpiece painted with broad strokes of intellectual curiosity and creative versatility.

23 Wednesday

As the Moon moves into Pisces, it brings a sense of sensitivity and heightened intuition to your emotional landscape. You may find yourself more attuned to the subtle nuances of your emotions and the energy around you. However, the challenging aspect of the Sun square Pluto adds intensity and potential power struggles to the mix. It's essential to be aware of any deep-seated fears, control issues, or power dynamics that may arise during this time.

24 Thursday

Gathering resources and cultivating support help you get busy manifesting your vision. A richly creative process is the crux of developing your abilities and nurturing your talents. You soon get active on a trail that inspires growth. It lets you remove any elements that are no longer relevant and head towards a journey that offers expansion and happiness. As you continue to attract positive results, the essence of manifestation surrounds your life.

25 Friday

Venus conjunct Saturn. Moon ingress Aries. This combination can create a dynamic tension between the need for stability and structure (Venus conjunct Saturn) and the desire for independence and personal freedom (Moon ingress Aries). It's essential to find a healthy balance between commitment and self-expression, recognizing the value of both in your relationships and personal growth.

26 Saturday

The cosmic spotlight shines on matters of security and stability, encouraging you to appreciate the simple pleasures of home. The Taurus Sun invites you to celebrate familial bonds with a nurturing and grounded approach, creating a sense of warmth and belonging. Under this celestial influence, the hearth of your home becomes a sanctuary of comfort, where the enduring qualities of Taurus infuse the atmosphere with tranquility and appreciation for the tangible joys of family life.

27 Sunday

As Mars opposes Pluto, you may experience intense power struggles and conflicts in various areas of your life. This aspect can bring forth deep-seated desires, fears, and confrontations that challenge your sense of control and authority. It's essential to be aware of power dynamics and avoid engaging in manipulative or destructive behaviors. Instead, focus on channeling this energy into constructive outlets, such as self-reflection, personal growth, and transformative change.

MAY

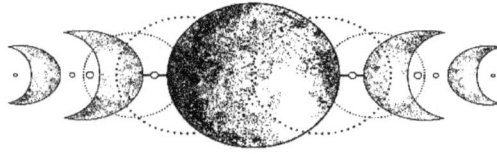

MOON MAGIC

Sun	Mon	Tue	Wed	Thu	Fri	Sat
				1	2	3
4	5	6	7	8	9	10
11	12	13	14	15	16	17
18	19	20	21	22	23	24
25	26	27	28	29	30	31

NEW MOON

FLOWER MOON

---

28 Monday

You can soon chart a course through a growth-orientated phase that draws harmony into your life. It clears up any issues clinging to your energy as it is restorative and therapeutic for your creative expression. It is an excellent time to step back and examine the path ahead as new areas are likely to come calling your name. A critical decision brings the opportunity to rebrand your image. It brings newfound possibilities that influence and inspire you to evolve and grow.

29 Tuesday

As the Moon enters Gemini, a curious and adaptable energy surrounds you, inviting you to explore the world with an open mind and a thirst for knowledge. This transit encourages you to embrace versatility and engage in stimulating conversations that broaden your perspective. You seek new information to satisfy your inquisitive nature. Gemini's influence enhances your communication skills, making expressing your thoughts and connecting with others easier.

30 Wednesday

As Venus enters Aries, you may feel a surge of passion and assertiveness in your relationships and desires. Aries brings a fiery and adventurous energy to your interactions, encouraging you to take charge and pursue what you truly want. You may be more inclined to express your desires and needs openly, without hesitation. This transit can inspire you to take bold action in matters of the heart and embrace a sense of independence in your relationships.

1 Thursday

Moon ingress Cancer. You might find solace in creating a cozy, harmonious atmosphere supporting your emotional well-being. Trust your intuition and listen to your inner voice as it guides you toward creating emotional balance and stability. This transit encourages you to connect with your loved ones on a deeper, more intimate level, fostering a sense of closeness and emotional connection. Allow yourself to be vulnerable and open, nurturing with love and compassion.

MAY

2 Friday

Venus conjunct Neptune. You may feel inspired to explore creative pursuits, whether it's through art, music, or simply finding beauty in the world around you. Embrace the gentle waves of Venus conjunct Neptune, allowing yourself to open up to the magic and wonder that exists both within and outside you. Let your heart guide you as you navigate this dreamy and introspective energy, and trust in the power of love and imagination to uplift and inspire your journey.

3 Saturday

You may notice a shift in your emotional landscape when the Moon moves into Leo. Your inner light shines brightly, and you naturally feel inclined to express yourself with confidence and enthusiasm. This lunar transit encourages you to embrace individuality and bask in the spotlight. You may find yourself seeking creative outlets to showcase your talents and seeking validation for your unique contributions.

4 Sunday

In the cosmic ballet, the powerful and transformative planet Pluto takes center stage as it begins its retrograde journey. As this celestial force appears to move backward in its orbit from our Earthly perspective, its energy becomes introspective and intense. Pluto, the ruler of the underworld in astrology, prompts us to delve deep into the recesses of our psyches, unearthing buried truths and hidden desires.

5 Monday

When Mercury forms a sextile aspect with Jupiter, you may experience a boost in your mental abilities and communication skills. This harmonious alignment encourages positive thinking, expanded perspectives, and optimism. Your mind is open to new possibilities, and you may find yourself enthusiastically seeking knowledge, learning, and exploring different subjects. It's a good time for making plans, setting goals, and envisioning a brighter future.

6 Tuesday

When Venus forms a sextile aspect with Pluto, you may experience a deepening of your emotional connections and a sense of passion and intensity in your relationships. This harmonious alignment invites transformative experiences in love, intimacy, and personal growth. You may seek to explore the depths of your emotions and forge meaningful connections with others. This aspect encourages you to express your authentic self with confidence and vulnerability.

7 Wednesday

Beautiful symmetry is coming into your life, which helps nurture grounded foundations. It brings a highly creative and expressive time that enables you to set sail on a voyage of your creation. Working with your creativity offers happiness and self-improvement, guiding you towards growing your talents. Extending your reach and listening to your instincts opens a journey that grows a positive chapter in your life.

8 Thursday

As the Moon gracefully glides into the charming and balanced sign of Libra, a shift in the cosmic energies invites us to embrace themes of harmony, diplomacy, and aesthetic appreciation. Libra, ruled by Venus, imparts a touch of grace and elegance to the lunar landscape, encouraging us to seek beauty and balance in our emotional experiences. This lunar ingress infuses your energy with a sense of balance, beauty, and a desire for connection.

9 Friday

Your life is ripening with fresh possibilities, drawing rising prospects into your sphere. A sense of anticipation suggests that something new is poised to blossom. Embracing the prospect of growing your world in a new direction promises a meaningful journey forward. Opportunities to engage with your social circle abound, heightening social engagement and deepening bonds with those who hold significance in your life.

10 Saturday

As Mercury moves into Taurus and the Moon enters Scorpio, you may experience a shift in your mental focus and emotional intensity. With Mercury in Taurus, your thoughts become more grounded and practical, and you may find yourself seeking stability and security in your communication style. Meanwhile, with the Moon in Scorpio, your emotions run deep, and you may find yourself delving into the depths of your inner world.

11 Sunday

In the heart of your home and family, Mercury in Taurus bestows a sense of stability and warmth to your Mother's Day celebrations. Feel the nurturing energy as Mercury invites you to express your feelings with sincerity and steadfastness. Under this celestial influence, your words become anchors of emotional support, fostering an atmosphere of comfort and understanding. Mercury in Taurus encourages expressions of love and appreciation today.

12 Monday

During the Full Moon, the intensity and emotional energy peak, illuminating areas requiring attention and transformation. This decisive lunar phase coincides with Mercury square Pluto, creating a dynamic tension between your thoughts and the depths of your subconscious. You may grapple with intense ideas and communications that carry transformative energy. It's a time to be cautious of power struggles, manipulations, and obsessive thinking patterns.

13 Tuesday

As the Moon enters Sagittarius, you may feel a surge of adventurous energy and a desire for exploration. Your focus shifts toward expanding your horizons, both intellectually and experientially. This transit is a time to seek new knowledge, broaden your perspectives, and embrace freedom. You are inspired to embark on new adventures, whether it's through travel, learning, or engaging in stimulating conversations with others.

14 Wednesday

Information on the horizon contributes to building more grounded foundations in your life. Discovering an area that fuels your emotional well-being adds a vibrant hue to your existence. Life takes on a lighter tone as blossoming activity attracts fresh options. This developmental journey offers room for growth along a unique path forward. It provides a platform to express your talents creatively, effectively fostering personal and professional development.

15 Thursday

Moon ingress Capricorn. You may find yourself motivated to work hard, make long-term plans, and take steps toward achieving your objectives. The energy of Capricorn encourages you to be organized, diligent, and determined in your pursuits. You may feel a stronger sense of self-discipline and a desire to establish a solid foundation for your future success. It's a time to prioritize your responsibilities, set realistic goals, and take calculated steps toward aspirations.

16 Friday

In the realm of communication and intellectual pursuits, Venus in Aries adds a touch of boldness and assertiveness to your interactions. Conversations become lively as the cosmic diplomat traverses the energetic landscape of Aries. Venus encourages you to express affection and appreciation with courage and spontaneity. Your connections may take on a dynamic and adventurous quality, and you may find joy in sharing ideas that reflect the fearless spirit of Aries.

17 Saturday

Sun conjunct Uranus alignment can ignite creativity and inspiration, urging you to explore new possibilities and push the boundaries. It's a time to embrace change and welcome the unexpected openly. Trust your intuition and allow your authentic self to shine brightly. Be open to the opportunities that arise, even if they challenge your comfort zone. Remember that embracing individuality and following your path can lead to exciting discoveries and personal growth.

18 Sunday

When Mercury squares Mars, there is a potential for intense mental and communicative energy. It may feel like your thoughts and words hold urgency and assertiveness. This aspect can bring forth a strong desire to express yourself and defend your ideas, but it's essential to be mindful of impulsive reactions and conflicts that may arise. With the Moon moving into Aquarius, you may feel a need for independence and a desire to break free from traditional constraints.

MAY

19 Monday

A fast-paced environment draws advancement into your life. You take disciplined action as you have the drive and perseverance to nail down the development of your dreams. You charge ahead towards more outstanding achievements by planning the path and setting intentions. Your dedication to improving life draws dividends as you pivot away from hurdles and channel your energy into developing an essential objective.

20 Tuesday

When the Sun forms a harmonious sextile aspect with Saturn, it brings a sense of stability, discipline, and practicality to your life. You may take a more structured and responsible approach to your goals and ambitions. This aspect supports long-term planning, organization, and the willingness to achieve objectives. It's a time to focus on building a solid foundation for your future success. With the Moon entering Pisces, you experience increased emotional sensitivity and intuition.

21 Wednesday

You discover new opportunities in life that shower over into your situation, which offer a rich and generous time to work with your creativity. It brings an extended time of growth, which heightens the sense of security in your life as you head towards transformation on many levels. A journey of rejuvenation brings an open road of possibility that tempts you forward. It helps you lay stable foundations that feel grounded and complete.

22 Thursday

When Venus forms a harmonious trine with Mars, it brings passion, harmony, and assertiveness to your relationships and personal desires. You may feel a strong magnetic attraction toward others, and there is a potential for romantic connections and creative collaborations to flourish. This aspect encourages you to express your desires confidently. With the Sun forming a sextile with Neptune, your life has a heightened imagination and spiritual awareness.

23 Friday

Changes act as catalysts, initiating a reboot in your life and creating ample opportunities to reconnect with friends. This transformative phase extends an invitation to broaden your horizons, sharing experiences and thoughts with others. The possibilities become vast, promoting lively conversations that foster social engagement and happiness. This period introduces a time of change and inspiration, elevating the goodness in your social life.

24 Saturday

When the Sun forms a harmonious trine with Pluto, it brings a powerful energy of transformation and empowerment to your life. This cosmic aspect encourages you to delve deep into your power, uncover hidden truths, and make positive changes. You may experience a heightened sense of self-awareness and the ability to overcome obstacles with resilience and determination. With the Moon entering Taurus, you are grounded and focused on practical matters.

25 Sunday

Saturn ingress Aries is a time to establish firm boundaries, take calculated risks, and embrace a sense of self-mastery. Saturn in Aries invites you to step into leadership positions, assert your independence, and build a solid foundation for your future endeavors. It's a period of personal growth and development where you can learn valuable lessons about self-reliance, accountability, and balancing your desires with your responsibilities to others.

26 Monday

With the Moon moving into Gemini, your emotions may align with your mental state, fostering a harmonious balance between your thoughts and feelings. This transit is a good time for effective communication, engaging in intellectual pursuits, and connecting with others through meaningful conversations. Harness the energy of this alignment to express yourself clearly, gather knowledge, and explore new perspectives.

27 Tuesday

During the New Moon, a fresh cycle begins, inviting you to set intentions and embark on new beginnings. With Mercury forming a harmonious trine with Pluto, your mind is deeply attuned to profound insights and transformative thinking. This alignment enhances your ability to delve into the depths of your thoughts and uncover hidden truths. You possess a heightened intuition and persuasive communication skills that can have a powerful impact on others.

28 Wednesday

Moon ingress Cancer. You may find solace in creative endeavors or spending time near bodies of water, as they have a soothing effect on your soul. Trust your intuition as you navigate the ebb and flow of your emotions, and allow yourself to seek the support and comfort you need. You can create a strong foundation for emotional well-being and inner harmony by honoring your dynamic emotional landscape during this Moon in Cancer.

29 Thursday

The upcoming opportunities align seamlessly with a refreshing period that encourages personal growth, advancement, and rising prospects. Delving into a new area becomes a winning formula, deepening your knowledge and refining your skills. This phase sparks inspiration, casting a light on your career path and revealing new possibilities that nurture growth. It marks an active time of leveraging your abilities.

JUNE

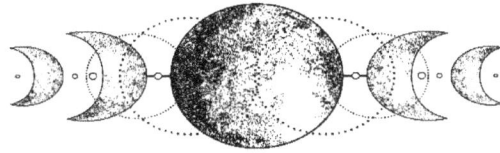

MOON MAGIC

Sun	Mon	Tue	Wed	Thu	Fri	Sat
1	2	3	4	5	6	7
8	9	10	11	12	13	14
15	16	17	18	19	20	21
22	23	24	25	26	27	28
29	30					

New Moon

STRAWBERRY MOON

_____

_____

_____

_____

_____

_____

_____

_____

_____

_____

_____

_____

_____

_____

_____

_____

_____

_____

_____

_____

30 Friday

With the Sun and Mercury coming together, there is a strong emphasis on communication, self-expression, and mental clarity. Your thoughts and ideas align with your sense of self, allowing you to articulate your thoughts with confidence and authenticity. As the Moon moves into Leo, you may feel a surge of creative energy and a desire to shine your light brightly. It is a time to embrace your unique voice and enthusiastically share your ideas and passions.

31 Saturday

Enter the cosmic realm of festivities, where the stars guide you in embracing the joyous dance of social connections and creative expression. Whether it's a brunch with friends or a themed artistic project, let the celestial energy infuse your day with a sense of magic and camaraderie. This cosmic period invites you to savor the beauty of shared moments and imaginative pursuits, creating moments filled with celestial brilliance.

1 Sunday

In the realm of creativity and self-expression, the Sun in Gemini energizes your fifth house with a playful and communicative flair. Your approach to artistic pursuits and romance becomes dynamic and versatile, reflecting the multifaceted nature of Gemini. Embrace the joy of self-expression through various creative outlets, reveling in the art of storytelling and the excitement of intellectual playfulness. The Sun invites you to shine brightly in matters of love and creativity.

2 Monday

As the Moon enters Virgo, you may notice a shift towards practicality and attention to detail in your life. You might find yourself drawn to organizing and improving your daily routines and seeking efficiency in your tasks and responsibilities. This transit is a time to focus on practical matters, health, and self-care. You may strongly desire to analyze and evaluate situations, seeking logical solutions to any challenges.

3 Tuesday

Anticipating cornerstone insights becomes a pivotal element in constructing more grounded foundations. Uncovering elements that fuel your emotional well-being imparts a lighter hue to life. Engaging in blossoming activities attracts a spectrum of new options, creating a developmental journey with ample room for growth along a unique and expressive path. As inspiration rises, it feeds motivation and provides you with energy that ignites innovative options worth your time.

4 Wednesday

As the Moon enters Libra, you may feel a heightened sense of balance, harmony, and a desire for peace in your interactions with others. This transit is when you naturally seek common ground, promote cooperation, and foster diplomacy in your relationships. You may find yourself more attuned to the needs and perspectives of those around you as you strive to create a harmonious atmosphere in your personal and professional connections.

5 Thursday

As Venus forms a sextile with Jupiter and Mercury forms a sextile with Mars, you will likely experience a harmonious and energizing influence. It is an auspicious time to explore new opportunities, expand your horizons, and engage in positive interactions. Your communication skills are enhanced, allowing you to express yourself with confidence and assertiveness. You may find yourself inspired to pursue your passions and take action toward your goals.

6 Friday

When Venus enters Taurus, it brings sensual and earthy energy into your life. You are drawn to the pleasures of the physical world, finding comfort and beauty in the simple things. This transit invites you to indulge in self-care and appreciate the abundance surrounding you. You may feel a stronger desire for stability and security in your relationships, valuing loyalty and commitment. Your aesthetic senses heighten, and you take pleasure in the finer details of life.

7 Saturday

When the Moon ingresses Scorpio, you may experience intense emotional energy. Your emotions become heightened and focused, and you may be delving into your feelings and desires. This transit is a time of transformation and regeneration, as Scorpio encourages you to let go of what no longer serves you and embrace the power of emotional healing. You may feel more introspective and inclined towards introspection and self-reflection.

8 Sunday

When Mercury conjuncts Jupiter and ingresses into Cancer, it offers the wisdom of your heart for you to communicate your feelings with clarity and depth. This alignment encourages you to explore new ideas and expand your knowledge, particularly in home, family, and emotional well-being. You may find yourself seeking meaningful conversations and connecting with others on a deeper level, sharing your insights and listening attentively to their experiences.

9 Monday

When Mercury squares Saturn, you may encounter communication and mental focus challenges. Staying patient and diligent in your thinking processes is essential, as this aspect can bring obstacles and delays. However, with the Moon's ingress into Sagittarius, you reveal an adventurous and optimistic spirit. You're able to tap into your inner wisdom and seek higher truths. This combination encourages expanding horizons and exploring new perspectives.

10 Tuesday

Embarking on the ascendancy trail aligns with a period of refreshing growth and advancement. Opportunities on the horizon weave seamlessly into a winning formula—learning a new area to deepen knowledge and skills. This inspirational chapter sheds light on your career path, uncovering possibilities that actively contribute to your personal and professional journey. Extending your reach into new areas draws dividends that take your trajectory higher.

11 Wednesday

Full Moon. Mercury sextile Venus. It's a time to appreciate the beauty around you and to express your creativity through words and gestures. Use this potent combination of the Full Moon and the harmonious Mercury-Venus aspect to nurture your relationships and express your true feelings with authenticity and compassion. It's a moment to embrace the power of love and communication and seek harmony and balance in your interactions.

12 Thursday

Moon ingress Capricorn. Capricorn's influence encourages emotional self-control and a focus on achieving tangible results. This lunar transit is favorable for setting realistic goals, making long-term plans, and taking a disciplined approach to emotional matters. It's a time when you may prioritize responsibilities and obligations, and there can be a sense of satisfaction in accomplishing tasks and meeting emotional commitments.

13 Friday

In the celestial realm on this Friday, the 13th, planetary movements create a dynamic and enigmatic dance. The cosmic energies suggest a day of subtle shifts and unexpected turns, inviting you to navigate with an open heart and a spirit of adaptability. Embrace the cosmic mysteries unfolding around you, recognizing the potential for both challenge and revelation on this uniquely charged day— surprise news, insightful opportunities, and avenues of growth open.

14 Saturday

As the Moon enters Aquarius, you may feel detached and inclined to embrace your individuality. Aquarius energy encourages you to step outside the norm and explore new ideas and perspectives. You feel inspired to contribute to your community or engage in social activism. You seek intellectual stimulation and engage in conversations that challenge your conventional thinking. This planetary alignment is a time to embrace your uniqueness and celebrate your authenticity.

15 Sunday

When Mars squares Uranus and Jupiter squares Saturn, you may experience a clash between freedom and the demands of responsibility. Uranus brings unexpected and disruptive energy, while Mars fuels desires for independence and assertiveness. On the other hand, Saturn represents structure and stability, while Jupiter expands ambitions and beliefs. This combination creates tension between wanting to break free and the need to abide by rules and limitations.

16 Monday

When the Moon enters Pisces, you find yourself in a world of emotions and heightened sensitivity. Pisces is a compassionate and intuitive sign, inviting you to dive deep into your inner world and connect with your subconscious. During this time, you may feel more empathetic and attuned to the feelings of others, which can foster a sense of unity and compassion. It's a good time for introspection, self-reflection, and exploring your creative and spiritual side.

17 Tuesday

When Mars ingresses Virgo, you have plenty of practical and diligent energy. Virgo is an earth sign that values efficiency, attention to detail, and a systematic task approach. During this time, you may feel motivated to tackle your to-do list, organize your surroundings, and improve your daily routines. Your focus and determination heighten, allowing you to progress significantly in your work and personal projects.

18 Wednesday

When the Moon ingresses Aries, you may feel a surge of energy and enthusiasm. Aries is a fire sign known for assertiveness, courage, and drive. You are motivated to take action, pursue your passions, and assert your individuality during this time. You desire to start new projects, take risks, and embrace challenges. Your confidence and determination heighten and attract activities requiring courage and initiative.

19 Thursday

Jupiter's square Neptune aspect invites you to question your beliefs, reassess your goals, and find a balance between optimism and practicality. Use this time to understand better your dreams and how they align with the practical aspects of life. By grounding your visions and taking reasonable steps toward your goals, you can navigate this transit with wisdom and integrity, allowing the tension between Jupiter and Neptune to inspire you to manifest your dreams tangibly.

20 Friday

In the cosmic ballet of celestial energies, today's spotlight falls on the intricate tapestry of relationship dynamics. Open up channels of communication, allowing the free flow of emotions and fostering a deeper understanding. The celestial alignment acts as a gentle guide, encouraging harmonious interactions. It's an ideal period to address any lingering conflicts, offering a chance for resolution and the cultivation of more profound emotional bonds that stand the test of time.

21 Saturday

Moon ingress Taurus. Sun ingress Cancer. June Solstice. This period encourages you to honor your roots, cherish your loved ones, and embrace a slower pace that allows for introspection and emotional healing. It's an opportunity to align with nature's rhythms and find joy and fulfillment in simple pleasures. Embrace the transformative energies of this season and allow yourself to blossom and thrive in the nurturing embrace of the Sun and Moon.

22 Sunday

While the Mars and Jupiter aspect fuels your drive, the Sun-Saturn aspect reminds you to approach your endeavors with wisdom, perseverance, and a structured plan. By combining your optimistic energy with careful consideration of the obstacles, you can navigate challenges and achieve long-term success. Embrace the lessons and opportunities from this cosmic interplay, and let them shape you into a stronger, more resilient version of yourself.

23 Monday

With the Moon moving into Gemini, there is a shift in your emotional landscape, bringing a sense of curiosity and mental agility. You may be more intellectually stimulated and eager to engage in lively conversations and explore new ideas. However, it's essential to navigate the Sun's square aspect to Neptune cautiously. This aspect can create confusion and uncertainty, making it challenging to see things clearly or make concrete decisions.

24 Tuesday

With the Sun aligning with Jupiter in conjunction, you surge with the powerful energy of expansion, optimism, and abundance. This cosmic alignment invites you to step into your greatness and embrace opportunities for growth and success. You may feel heightened confidence and enthusiasm, encouraging you to aim high and believe in your abilities. The Sun's conjunction with Jupiter empowers you to take action, seize the day, and pursue your dreams with renewed purpose.

25 Wednesday

With the Moon entering Cancer and the arrival of a New Moon, a fresh cycle begins, offering you a powerful opportunity for emotional renewal and setting new intentions. You may feel sensitivity and a heightened awareness of your needs. You can tune into your feelings and nurture your inner world, creating a solid foundation for growth and transformation. The New Moon in Cancer invites you to connect with your emotional needs and establish security and comfort.

26 Thursday

As the Sun forms a sextile with Mars, you have the energy and motivation to pursue your passions. This harmonious aspect empowers you to take confident and decisive action, fueling your drive. With Mercury moving into Leo, your self-expression becomes bolder and more confident, encouraging you to speak from the heart and let your unique personality shine. The dynamic energy of these aspects inspires you to think innovatively and take bold steps toward your desires.

27 Friday

Moon ingress Leo. Embrace the spirit of playfulness and spontaneity, and let your inner child come out to play. Surround yourself with positive and supportive people who uplift and inspire you. Use this lunar energy to set bold intentions and pursue your dreams enthusiastically and determinedly. Remember, you can create a life that reflects your true essence. Embrace the Leo Moon's radiant energy and let it fuel your self-expression and personal growth journey.

28 Saturday

Mercury forms a harmonious trine aspect with Saturn and Neptune, bringing a beautiful blend of practicality and imagination into your life. You find yourself in mental clarity and focus, enabling you to make well-grounded decisions and communicate effectively. Your thoughts feel organized, and you can bring structure and discipline to your ideas. At the same time, the trine to Neptune opens the door to your creative and intuitive faculties.

29 Sunday

Mercury-opposed Pluto alignment can bring intense mental energy and a strong desire to uncover hidden truths and delve into the depths of your psyche. You may deeply introspect and question your life's motives and power dynamics. With the Moon entering Virgo, you may find solace in organizing and attending to the details of your daily life. It helps you navigate the intensity of the Mercury-Pluto opposition by grounding your thoughts and seeking practical solutions.

July

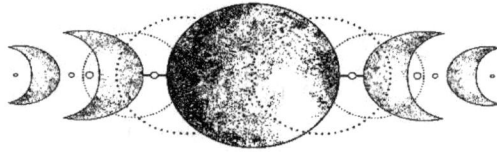

MOON MAGIC

Sun	Mon	Tue	Wed	Thu	Fri	Sat
		1	2	3	4	5
6	7	8	9	10	11	12
13	14	15	16	17	18	19
20	21	22	23	24	25	26
27	28	29	30	31		

AQUARIUS

NEW MOON

BUCK MOON

---

30 Monday

In the cosmic landscape of daily routines and work, the Sun in Cancer illuminates your sixth house, infusing your tasks with nurturing and protective energy. Your approach to day-to-day responsibilities becomes deeply tied to your emotional well-being, and you find satisfaction in creating a harmonious and caring work environment. Embrace the joy of nurturing others through your work, finding fulfillment in tasks that contribute to the well-being of those around you.

1 Tuesday

When the Moon enters Libra, you are likely to experience a shift towards seeking harmony and balance in your emotional landscape. This transit encourages you to focus on your relationships and how to create a sense of equilibrium in your interactions with others. You may find yourself more attuned to the needs and perspectives of those around you, fostering a greater sense of empathy and understanding as you seek environments and experiences that inspire and uplift.

2 Wednesday

Amidst the cosmic symphony, a crescendo of energy directs your attention to the temple of well-being. Embrace the celestial energies, encouraging heightened mindfulness in your daily routine. Consider integrating practices such as meditation, yoga, or mindful eating to nurture both your physical and mental health. This reasonable time serves as a call to prioritize self-care, fostering a sense of balance and vitality that resonates through every facet of your existence.

3 Thursday

Navigating blossoming frontiers becomes an exploratory journey, offering opportunities to reconnect with friends and share thoughts and experiences. This rebooted phase unfolds as an expansive exploration of broader possibilities, fostering conversations that bring joy and engagement to your social life. This period of change and inspiration emphasizes the goodness that emerges from connecting with others.

4 Friday

When the Moon enters Scorpio, you may experience intense emotional energy. This astrological transit invites you to delve into the depths of your emotions and explore your innermost desires. With Venus conjunct Uranus, unexpected and exciting changes may occur in relationships or finances. It's a time of liberation and freedom, where you may feel inspired to break free from old patterns and embrace new and unconventional forms of love and self-expression.

5 Saturday

In the transformative eighth house, Mars in Virgo indicates a dynamic and analytical approach to matters of shared resources, intimacy, and regeneration. Your energy is directed toward deepening connections and understanding the underlying dynamics of joint ventures. You may be assertive in matters of joint finances and exhibit a keen interest in investigating hidden truths. Your ability to channel energy into transformative processes can lead to personal growth.

6 Sunday

With the Moon entering Sagittarius, you feel a sense of adventure and a thirst for knowledge. This transit inspires you to broaden your horizons, explore new ideas, and seek meaningful experiences. You may feel renewed optimism and enthusiasm, fueling your desire for growth and expansion in all areas of your life. Embrace this optimistic and creative energy, allowing it to guide you on self-discovery and connection with others.

7 Monday

With Uranus entering Gemini, a dynamic and intellectually stimulating energy is infused into your life. This transit encourages change as you explore new ideas and break traditional patterns. It sparks curiosity and innovation, inspiring you to think outside the box and pursue unconventional paths. As Venus forms a trine with Pluto, powerful and transformative energy is at play. This aspect brings deep emotional connections, intense passion, and the potential for transformation.

8 Tuesday

The Sun in Cancer gracing your sixth house brings a sense of emotional dedication and attentiveness to your professional life. Your daily tasks are not just chores but expressions of your commitment to the well-being of yourself and those around you. The Sun in this placement encourages you to infuse your work environment with a sense of nurturing and support, making it a space where the emotional needs of both yourself and your colleagues are recognized.

9 Wednesday

With the Moon entering Capricorn, you can embrace a sense of stability, responsibility, and determination in your emotional and practical endeavors. This transit encourages you to focus on your long-term goals, take charge of your life, and cultivate a disciplined approach to achieving success. You may find yourself more driven, organized, and ambitious during this time as you strive to create a solid foundation for your personal and professional life.

10 Thursday

The Full Moon is an opportunity to release anything that no longer serves you and make space for new beginnings. Allow yourself to fully embrace the energy of the Full Moon, engage in self-reflection, and take actions that align with your inner truth. Use this time to gain clarity, make decisions, and manifest positive changes in your life. Trust in the process and let the Full Moon guide you toward greater self-awareness and personal growth.

11 Friday

When the Moon moves into Aquarius, you may feel a shift in your emotional energy. Aquarius is an air sign known for its intellectual and forward-thinking nature. During this time, you may feel a deeper connection to social causes, humanitarian endeavors, and innovative ideas. You may feel a stronger sense of independence and a desire to express your individuality. It's a time to embrace your uniqueness and explore new perspectives.

12 Saturday

In the fifth house, Venus in Gemini influences your approach to creativity, romance, and self-expression. You express love and affection through lively conversations, intellectual pursuits, and playful activities. Your romantic interests are often sparked by mental connection and shared interests. Creatively, you may find joy in diverse forms of artistic expression and enjoy exploring new hobbies and activities.

13 Sunday

When Saturn turns retrograde, it invites you to reflect on your responsibilities, commitments, and long-term goals. This cosmic aspect is a time for introspection and review, where you can assess the structures and limitations in your life. You may need to reassess your priorities and make necessary adjustments to align with your true purpose and inner wisdom. With the Moon entering Pisces, your emotions may become more sensitive and intuitive.

14 Monday

Amidst the cosmic dance, the universe unfurls a canvas of innovative inspirations. This cosmic alignment invites you to tap into the boundless well of creative energy surrounding you. Whether you find yourself working on a project, seeking inventive solutions in business, or cultivating a mindset of continuous innovation, allow the celestial forces to ignite your imaginative endeavors. This dance beckons you to align with the celestial rhythm, unlocking new dimensions of productivity.

15 Tuesday

Today's celestial alignment navigates you through the constellations of finance. Planetary shifts bring forth a cosmic map to guide your financial decisions. Take this cosmic navigation as an opportunity to review investments, budgeting strategies, and financial goals. Allow the celestial compass to steer you towards a path of financial stability and abundance. It is a moment to align your financial choices with the ebb and flow of cosmic energies.

16 Wednesday

You may experience renewed energy surge and enthusiasm when the Moon enters Aries. This fiery and assertive energy ignites your passion and drive, encouraging you to take bold and decisive actions. It's a time to embrace new beginnings and assert your individuality. You may feel a strong urge to initiate projects, pursue your goals, and maintain yourself in various areas of life. Trust your instincts and let your inner fire guide you toward what excites and inspires you.

17 Thursday

As the planets align in the cosmic dance, their focus turns towards the realms of finance. Planetary shifts bring forth valuable insights into your monetary landscape, encouraging a meticulous review of budgets, investments, and financial goals. Seize this cosmic guidance as an opportunity to make informed decisions, ensuring the stability and growth of your financial future. Align your financial compass with your long-term goals for a prosperous journey.

18 Friday

Mercury turns retrograde. As the Moon moves into Taurus, you're encouraged to ground yourself and focus on stability and practicality. It is a favorable time for nurturing relationships and finding comfort in familiar surroundings. With Mercury sextile Venus, you can enhance your communication skills and express yourself with grace and charm. Take advantage of this alignment to strengthen your connections with others and find harmony in your interactions.

19 Saturday

In the seventh house, Mercury in Leo influences your approach to partnerships, relationships, and one-on-one interactions. You express yourself with warmth and enthusiasm in your connections with others, valuing open communication and mutual respect. Your conversations are lively and engaging, and you may seek partners who appreciate your charismatic and confident communication style. Strive for a balanced and cooperative approach in your relationships.

20 Sunday

As the Moon moves into Gemini, it infuses your emotional landscape with curiosity and intellectual stimulation. It is when your mind is sharp and you're eager to engage in conversations and explore new ideas. Your interest may lead you to seek diverse experiences and gather information from various sources. Embrace Gemini energy's versatility and adaptability, allowing yourself to embrace different perspectives and expand your knowledge.

21 Monday

Today's cosmic alignment unveils a celestial stage for reflections and advancements within your professional journey. The planetary shifts offer profound insights into the trajectory of your career. It is an opportune moment to harness the vast currents of universal inspiration guiding your endeavors. Whether contemplating new opportunities, setting goals, or envisioning the expansive landscape of your professional future, let the cosmic forces be your guiding light.

22 Tuesday

Moon ingress Cancer. Sun ingress Leo. Use this combination of Cancer's sensitivity and Leo's self-expression to honor your emotions and express yourself with authenticity and warmth. Focus on nurturing your relationships and finding creative outlets that allow you to share your unique gifts with the world. Allow your inner light to radiate and bring positivity to your personal and creative endeavors.

23 Wednesday

Sun sextile Uranus aspect encourages you to explore new possibilities and step outside of your comfort zone. You are presented with opportunities for personal growth and self-discovery, allowing you to express your individuality and break free from old patterns. It's a time to be open-minded, flexible, and adaptable to unexpected circumstances. However, the square between Venus and Mars brings a dynamic and potentially challenging energy to your relationships and desires.

24 Thursday

As the New Moon arrives, it signals a fresh start, a blank canvas upon which you can paint your desires and set new intentions. It is a powerful time for self-reflection, envisioning your future, and planting the seeds of growth. Embrace the supportive energy of the Sun trine Saturn and Sun trine Neptune, along with the transformative power of the New Moon, to step into a new chapter of your life with confidence and a deep sense of purpose.

25 Friday

Sun-opposed Pluto aspect can bring forth deep transformations and uncover hidden parts of your personality. It's a time of introspection and self-reflection as you confront your fears and desires. You may encounter situations that force you to abandon old patterns and beliefs that no longer serve you. This opposition can catalyze growth and empowerment if you are willing to face your inner demons and embrace your power.

26 Saturday

Moon ingress Virgo. Your analytical and discerning abilities heighten, allowing you to approach things with a precise and methodical mindset. You may find yourself drawn to routines, structure, and taking care of your physical well-being. It's a favorable time for work, productivity, and getting things in order. Take advantage of this energy to tackle tasks or projects requiring precision and attention to detail.

27 Sunday

Enter the cosmic realm where the stars guide you in embracing the joyous dance of imaginative expression. Whether it's a themed artistic project or a creative endeavor with friends, let the celestial energy infuse your days with a sense of magic. Embrace creating a symphony where artistic expressions create moments filled with cosmic brilliance. This cosmic period invites you to savor the beauty of collaborative creativity, creating moments filled with celestial brilliance.

28 Monday

Today's celestial alignment unveils a cosmic celebration of connection. Immerse yourself in the cosmic symphony of interactions. Whether engaging in conversations, exploring new connections, or savoring the beauty of communication, let the universal energies be your guide. It is a moment to celebrate the diverse ways in which connections unfold in the cosmic dance of life. Allow the celestial energies to guide the strengthening of bonds in your life.

29 Tuesday

Moon ingress Libra. You may also feel drawn to artistic and creative pursuits, finding beauty and inspiration in the world around you. Use this transit to cultivate peace and equilibrium and foster connections with others based on mutual respect and understanding. Embrace the energy of Libra to bring more grace and diplomacy into your interactions and promote unity and collaboration in your social circles.

30 Wednesday

Today's cosmic energies invite you on an enchanting exploration of the realms of flow and effortless engagement. Whether you find yourself immersed in work, creative endeavors, or daily routines, let the universal currents guide you into a state of sublime flow. Embrace the natural rhythm of tasks and activities, allowing the cosmic forces to facilitate a sense of ease and harmony in your pursuits. Whether your goals are personal or professional, let the cosmic inspire your effort.

31 Thursday

With the Sun conjunct Mercury, your communication skills improve, allowing you to express your thoughts and feelings with clarity and confidence. This alignment supports open and honest conversations, making it an excellent time for discussing your emotions and desires with loved ones. Use this powerful cosmic energy to cultivate meaningful connections and strengthen your emotional bonds with others.

AUGUST

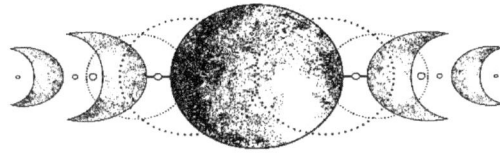

MOON MAGIC

Sun	Mon	Tue	Wed	Thu	Fri	Sat
					1	2
3	4	5	6	7	8	9
10	11	12	13	14	15	16
17	18	19	20	21	22	23
24	25	26	27	28	29	30
31						

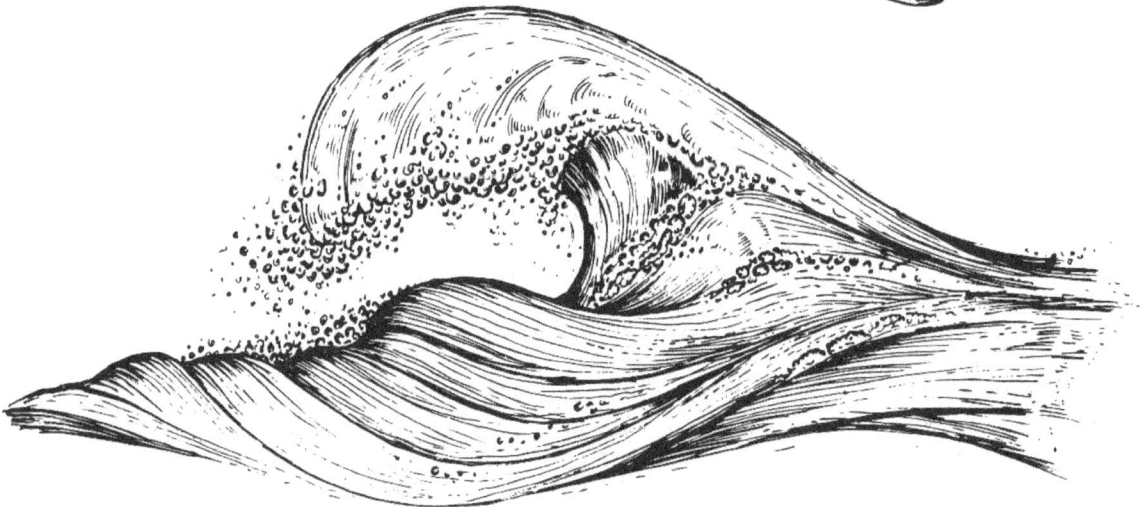

NEW MOON

_____

_____

_____

_____

_____

_____

_____

_____

_____

_____

_____

_____

_____

_____

_____

_____

_____

_____

_____

_____

Sturgeon Moon

1 Friday

When Venus forms a square with Saturn, you may experience a sense of restriction or limitation in your relationships or finances. It could feel like obstacles or challenges in expressing love or receiving affection. This aspect may lead to feelings of insecurity or a need for validation. Simultaneously, with Venus square Neptune, there is a potential for confusion or idealization in matters of love and attraction.

2 Saturday

The radiant Sun in Leo illuminates your seventh house of partnerships, bringing warm and theatrical energy to your relationships. You are drawn to dynamic, expressive partners who appreciate your grand gestures of love. Your desire for recognition and admiration is often fulfilled through your significant connections, and you approach partnerships with a sense of pride and loyalty. However, it's essential to balance the spotlight, ensuring bonds are valued and appreciated.

3 Sunday

Moon ingress Sagittarius. Your mind may expand with curiosity, and you'll seek new experiences and knowledge. This transit can bring enthusiasm and a desire to explore different cultures, beliefs, and philosophies. You may feel more open-minded and willing to embrace opportunities for growth and learning. Embrace the adventurous spirit within you and use this time to broaden your horizons and discover new perspectives.

4 Monday

Beneath the intricate threads of the cosmic tapestry, immerse yourself in the dynamic currents of productivity. Feel the subtle guidance of universal energies as you navigate through tasks, unlocking a seamless flow that enhances efficiency and accomplishment. This celestial alignment isn't just a dance of productivity; it's a symphony where your actions find synchronicity with the cosmic rhythm, propelling you towards a crescendo of achievements and fulfillment.

5 Tuesday

Moon ingress Capricorn's an excellent time to set clear intentions and work steadily towards your objectives. The Capricorn influence may also inspire you to reflect on long-term plans and how to achieve lasting success. Embrace the sense of maturity and perseverance that comes with this lunar phase, and use it to make progress in areas that are important to you. Remember to balance your ambitions with self-care and take time to nurture your emotional well-being.

6 Wednesday

Mars ingress Libra. Embrace a more graceful and diplomatic way of expressing your desires and passions to create win-win situations. Remember that finding common ground and fostering understanding will lead to smoother and more productive interactions with those around you. Stay open-minded and approach situations with a focus on collaboration, and you'll navigate this period with grace and finesse.

7 Thursday

Today's celestial alignment unfurls a cosmic celebration of social opportunities and bonds. Immerse yourself in the cosmic symphony of interactions, where business and personal connections alike take center stage. Let the universal energies guide you in fostering meaningful relationships that align with the cosmic rhythms. It is a celebration where social bonds become an integral part of the dance of life.

8 Friday

Moon ingress Aquarius. Mars trine Uranus. It's a great time to connect with like-minded individuals and engage in thought-provoking discussions that expand your horizons. Your intuition heightens, leading you to discover inventive solutions to challenges or opportunities for personal growth. Embrace the spirit of adventure and let your curiosity lead as the Moon in Aquarius and the Mars-Uranus trine open doors to exciting and unexpected possibilities.

9 Saturday

You may grapple with conflicting energies and emotions, with Mars opposing Saturn and Neptune and the Full Moon illuminating the skies. Mars opposing Saturn can create tension and frustration, making asserting yourself and achieving your goals challenging. You might encounter obstacles and delays that test your patience and determination. The Full Moon's influence brings emotions to the surface, intensifying feelings and stirring inner conflicts.

10 Sunday

With the Moon entering Pisces and Mars forming a trine with Pluto, you may experience emotional depth and intensity. The Moon in Pisces enhances your intuition and compassion, encouraging you to connect profoundly with your emotions and those of others. It's a time to tap into your creative and imaginative side, allowing inspiration to flow freely. Meanwhile, the harmonious aspect between Mars and Pluto empowers you with determination to pursue your goals.

11 Monday

As Mercury turns direct, you can expect a shift in communication and mental clarity. After a retrograde period, things may fall into place, and misunderstandings or delays could resolve. It is an excellent time to move forward with plans, make important decisions, and engage in open and honest conversations. You might notice that your thoughts are more straightforward, and communication flows more smoothly.

12 Tuesday

With Saturn sextile Uranus, you experience a harmonious blend of stability and innovation. This aspect encourages you to embrace change and progress while appreciating the importance of structure and discipline. It's a favorable time to explore unconventional approaches, and the ability to balance tradition with modernity can lead to exciting opportunities. Additionally, with Venus conjunct Jupiter, your social and romantic life could see an upswing of abundance.

13 Wednesday

Within the cosmic expanse, a radiant galaxy unfolds, teeming with networking opportunities that sparkle like distant stars. Embrace the cosmic constellations that guide you, illuminating a path to forge meaningful connections. This dance transforms networking into a celestial journey, where the threads of relationships weave into a tapestry, resonating with the timeless energies of the universe. Engage in this cosmic ballet and witness the beauty of interconnectedness.

14 Thursday

As the Moon enters Taurus, you may notice a shift towards a more grounded and stable emotional state. This influence encourages you to seek comfort, security, and pleasure in your surroundings. You might find yourself drawn to activities that promote relaxation and enjoyment, such as spending time in nature, indulging in delicious food, or engaging in creative pursuits. It is a favorable time to focus on practical matters and tend to physical and emotional well-being.

15 Friday

Mercury's sextile Mars aspect also supports taking action on your plans and ideas, as you have the mental clarity and determination to push forward. Use this favorable energy to initiate meaningful conversations, make decisions, and get things done efficiently and effectively. Your ability to articulate your thoughts and intentions can lead to positive outcomes. Embrace this aspect's confident and assertive energy to achieve your goals and progress in various areas of your life.

16 Saturday

With the Moon ingressing Gemini, you may experience a shift in your emotional focus toward intellectual pursuits and social interactions. Your curiosity and desire for mental stimulation increase during this time, making it an excellent period for learning, exploring new ideas, and engaging in meaningful conversations. Your communication skills will be heightened, and you might be more expressive and adaptable in various social settings.

17 Sunday

Pioneering into a transformative odyssey brings forth moments of change, inviting connection with friends and the sharing of experiences. Life takes on the hues of a vibrant harvest, promising fresh possibilities that draw rising prospects into your sphere. Embracing the prospect of growing your world in a new direction sets the stage for a meaningful journey forward. It cultivates nurturing conversations that bring social engagement and happiness to the forefront.

18 Monday

Mercury's sextile Mars aspect encourages dynamic thinking and quick decision-making, empowering you to take action on your plans and goals. Meanwhile, with the Moon's ingress into Cancer, emotions become pronounced, fostering a stronger connection to home and family during this period. This combination of celestial events encourages you to blend your mental acuity with emotional understanding, enabling you to navigate with intelligence and compassion.

19 Tuesday

In the sixth house, Venus in Cancer influences your approach to work, daily routines, and health with a nurturing and empathetic touch. You find pleasure in creating a harmonious and supportive work environment, valuing cooperation and mutual understanding among colleagues. Your creativity may shine through in your daily tasks, and you may seek roles that allow you to express your caring and compassionate nature.

20 Wednesday

As the Moon enters Leo today, you may find a surge of passion and creativity within you. Leo's influence also brings a playful and adventurous spirit to your emotions, encouraging you to engage in joyful and exciting activities. Use this time to express yourself authentically and pursue your passions with courage and flair. The world is your stage, and under this lunar transit, you can feel destined to take center stage and captivate those around you.

21 Thursday

In the expansive ninth house, Mars in Libra influences your approach to travel, higher education, and philosophical pursuits with a desire for harmony and balanced assertiveness. You may assert yourself passionately in areas related to beliefs and values, seeking justice and fairness. Your energy is directed toward exploring diverse cultures and intellectual pursuits, often engaging in activities that involve collaboration and negotiation.

22 Friday

Sun ingress Virgo astrological event brings increased efficiency and a desire to organize and streamline aspects of your life. You might find yourself drawn to analyzing situations more critically and seeking ways to improve and refine your routines. This Earth sign influence encourages you to take a grounded and systematic approach to your goals, ensuring that you pay attention to the finer points and make tangible progress.

23 Saturday

New Moon. In the tranquil cosmic stillness, embark on a profound journey of strategic planning. The planetary shifts create a serene space for deliberate considerations, allowing you to craft plans that resonate with the cosmic frequencies. Take this cosmic moment to refine your strategies, set intentional goals, and envision your path into the future. Allow the universal energies to guide you in planning strategies that align with the grand cosmic design.

24 Sunday

Sun square Uranus' astrological aspect can generate a sense of restlessness and electric energy. You may feel compelled to shake things up and introduce excitement into your life. However, managing this energy is vital to avoiding impulsive actions. Uranus is associated with sudden insights and revelations. During this aspect, you may experience moments of clarity; remaining open-minded and willing to explore new perspectives can be transformative.

25 Monday

As the Moon enters Libra, you might seek more balance and harmony in your emotions and relationships. This lunar influence encourages you to be more diplomatic and considerate of others' perspectives, fostering a cooperative atmosphere. With Venus also moving into Leo, there's an added flair of creativity, passion, and self-expression in your romantic endeavors and personal pursuits. Embrace the playful qualities of Venus in Leo to add joy to your connections.

26 Tuesday

With Venus forming favorable aspects to Saturn, Uranus, and Neptune, you may experience emotional depth and stability in your relationships. The Venus trine Saturn aspect brings a sense of commitment and reliability to your love life, allowing you to build strong bonds. The Venus sextile Uranus influence adds a touch of excitement and novelty to your romantic interactions, introducing surprising and delightful experiences that can invigorate your connections.

27 Wednesday

Venus opposed Pluto's astrological aspect, which can bring forth hidden desires and issues of control, leading to potential conflicts. Be cautious of power struggles, as they could create tension and disrupt your connections with others. This opposition may also trigger transformational experiences in love and finance, urging you to confront deep-seated emotional patterns. Approach this time with self-awareness and a willingness to embrace change, which can lead to healing.

28 Thursday

As the Moon enters Scorpio, you might feel a shift in your emotions towards introspection. You may experience heightened intuition and a stronger connection to your instincts during this period. It's essential to allow yourself the space to process your emotions and delve into areas that may have been previously overlooked or suppressed. Embrace this potent lunar influence to gain insights into your inner world and use it to catalyze positive change and empowerment.

29 Friday

Uranus sextile Neptune astrological alignment can inspire you to think outside the box and explore new possibilities in various aspects of your life. Your imagination and creativity will likely amplify, making it an excellent time for artistic pursuits and spiritual exploration. This harmonious connection between Uranus and Neptune encourages you to embrace change with an open mind and a willingness to adapt to unconventional ideas.

30 Saturday

As the Moon enters Sagittarius, you may feel a surge of optimism and enthusiasm in your emotional landscape. Sagittarius' influence encourages you to seek new experiences and expand your horizons. You might yearn for adventure and a deeper understanding of the world around you. This lunar transit fosters a sense of curiosity and a desire for knowledge, making it an excellent time for learning, exploring different cultures, or engaging in philosophical discussions.

31 Sunday

In the profound and transformative eighth house, your Virgo Sun infuses your life with a sense of practicality and discernment in matters of shared resources and intimacy. You approach financial matters and intimate connections with a methodical and analytical mindset, seeking to create stability and order. Be cautious not to let worries about imperfection hinder the depth of your emotional connections, and embrace vulnerability for true transformation and growth.

S<small>EPTEMBER</small>

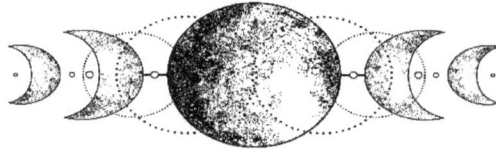

MOON MAGIC

Sun	Mon	Tue	Wed	Thu	Fri	Sat
	1	2	3	4	5	6
7	8	9	10	11	12	13
14	15	16	17	18	19	20
21	22	23	24	25	26	27
28	29	30				

NEW MOON

CORN/HARVEST MOON

_____

_____

_____

_____

_____

_____

_____

_____

_____

_____

_____

_____

_____

_____

_____

_____

_____

_____

SEPTEMBER

1 Monday

With Saturn's ingress into Pisces, you may feel a shift in your approach to discipline, responsibility, and spirituality. During this period, you might focus more on understanding the deeper meaning of life and exploring your inner world. Saturn's influence in Pisces encourages you to confront your emotional boundaries and address any unresolved issues from the past. You can work on releasing old patterns and emotional burdens that no longer serve you.

2 Tuesday

The Moon in Capricorn encourages discipline and goal-oriented actions, making it an excellent time for tackling tasks requiring determination and structure. Your emotions may feel more stable and grounded, allowing you to stay composed even in challenging situations. With Mercury in Virgo, your communication style becomes more analytical and detail-oriented. It is favorable for problem-solving and organizing your thoughts with precision.

3 Wednesday

With Mercury forming a square aspect to Uranus, you may experience a period of mental restlessness and a heightened desire for intellectual stimulation. This astrological influence can bring sudden insights and innovative ideas, leading to scattered thinking and impulsive decision-making. You might find yourself craving excitement and change in your thought processes, seeking alternative viewpoints and unconventional approaches to problem-solving.

4 Thursday

As the Moon enters Aquarius, you might experience a shift in your emotional landscape, embracing a more open and progressive mindset. Aquarius' influence encourages you to embrace your individuality and unique perspectives, fostering a sense of detachment from conventional norms. During this lunar transition, you may find yourself drawn to social causes and humanitarian endeavors as you seek to impact the world around you positively.

5 Friday

With Mars forming a square aspect to Jupiter, you may experience a surge of enthusiasm and a drive for action. This astrological influence can boost energy and confidence, making you eager to take on challenges and expand your horizons. However, be mindful of a tendency to be overly optimistic or impulsive during this time. It's crucial to balance your boldness with a practical approach and avoid overextending yourself or taking on more than you can handle.

6 Saturday

Uranus' retrograde planetary shift encourages you to look within and reassess areas where you may have sought independence, freedom, or radical changes. It's a time to review your past actions and decisions, considering whether they align with your authentic self and long-term goals. With the Moon's ingress into Pisces, your emotional sensitivity deepens, and you might find yourself more attuned to the subtleties of your feelings and the emotions of those around you.

7 Sunday

Full Moon is a time of heightened emotions, and you may feel more sensitive and attuned to your inner world. This lunar event can bring a sense of closure to projects or situations that have been ongoing while also presenting opportunities for releasing what no longer serves you. Embrace the Full Moon's transformative energy and use it as a time for reflection, releasing old patterns, and setting intentions for the next phase of your journey.

8 Monday

As the Moon moves into Aries, you may feel a surge of energy and assertiveness. This lunar transit brings a bold and adventurous spirit to your emotions, encouraging you to take the lead and pursue your passions with enthusiasm. You might be more impulsive and eager to explore new experiences or start fresh projects. It's a time to embrace your individuality and take decisive action in areas that have been stagnant or require a burst of motivation.

9 Tuesday

The cosmic constellations converge to illuminate a singular goal, casting a luminous beam onto your professional aspirations. Focus on this guiding light as it unveils a strategic path toward success. Trust the celestial map that unfolds, revealing stepping stones that lead to the fulfillment of your career dreams. Allow the stars to be your compass, guiding you with unwavering optimism toward the realization of your ambitions.

10 Wednesday

As the Moon enters Taurus, you may notice a shift towards a more grounded and stable emotional state. Taurus' influence brings comfort and a deeper appreciation for life's simple pleasures. During this lunar transition, you might seek security and harmony in your surroundings and relationships. This transit is a favorable time to indulge in sensory experiences and nurture yourself with the things that bring you comfort and joy.

11 Thursday

Today's cosmic dance invites you to explore the delicate balance between independence and connection. Feel the subtle nudges of universal energies guiding you to maintain autonomy while fostering meaningful connections with others. This celestial alignment encourages a dance where you embrace your individuality within the interconnected web of your relationships, finding harmony in the ebb and flow of independence and connection.

12 Friday

With the Sun forming a sextile aspect to Jupiter, you experience optimism and confidence, enhancing your aspirations. This cosmic alignment encourages you to seek opportunities for growth and expansion in various areas of your life. As the Moon moves into Gemini, your emotions may become more adaptable and communicative, fostering a curiosity for learning and social interactions. This lunar transit promotes mental agility and a desire for intellectual stimulation.

13 Saturday

Sun conjunct Mercury. Your mind is sharp, and you may find yourself full of new insights and innovative solutions to problems. This cosmic transit is an excellent time for learning and engaging in meaningful discussions, as your ability to absorb information and communicate effectively is at its peak. Embrace this harmonious union of the Sun and Mercury to express yourself confidently and make the most of this intellectually stimulating period.

14 Sunday

Embrace practices that nurture both your physical and mental well-being, creating a harmonious balance in the cosmic dance of life. Whether adopting new wellness rituals, exploring invigorating fitness routines, or cultivating mindful habits, let the cosmic energies compose a symphony of vitality and equilibrium in your daily existence. Today is a cosmic invitation to integrate wellness practices seamlessly into the rhythm of your life, fostering a holistic sense of well-being.

15 Monday

Moon ingress Cancer. Cancer's influence brings a sense of nurturing and sensitivity, prompting you to connect more deeply with your feelings and the emotions of those around you. During this lunar transit, you might feel a more substantial need for security and a desire to create a comforting and supportive environment. This transit is a favorable time for bonding with family and loved ones and taking care of yourself emotionally.

16 Tuesday

Venus sextile Mars is an ideal time to express your feelings and desires, as communication attracts warmth and receptivity. The Venus-Mars sextile also promotes creative and romantic endeavors, making it an opportune time to explore your artistic talents or deepen your connections with a partner. Embrace the harmonious energies of this aspect to embrace a period of loving and exciting interactions, fostering camaraderie and appreciation in your relationships.

17 Wednesday

You may experience a heightened desire for recognition and self-expression as the Moon moves into Leo. Leo's influence brings a sense of confidence and showmanship, encouraging you to seek the spotlight and share your creative ideas with others. However, with Mercury opposed to Saturn, you might encounter mental challenges and obstacles in your communication. This aspect can lead to self-doubt and a sense of limitation in expressing yourself effectively.

18 Thursday

As Mercury moves into Libra, you may seek greater harmony and balance in your communication style. This astrological influence encourages you to be more diplomatic and considerate of others' viewpoints, fostering a cooperative and fair exchange of ideas. However, with Mercury opposing Neptune, there's a potential for confusion and miscommunication. Your thoughts and perceptions may become clouded, leading to misunderstandings and unrealistic expectations.

19 Friday

With Mercury forming trines to Uranus and Pluto, your mind may feel exceptionally sharp and insightful during this period. The trine to Uranus enhances your capacity for innovative thinking and intellectual curiosity, making it an excellent time for learning and exploring new ideas. Simultaneously, the trine to Pluto strengthens your ability to delve into deeper layers of understanding, uncovering hidden truths and transforming your perceptions.

20 Saturday

Venus Square Uranus. It's crucial to stay open-minded, embrace the unexpected, and be cautious of making hasty choices that could have long-term consequences. Use this time to explore your individuality and discover what indeed resonates with you on a deeper level. By finding a balance between spontaneity and stability, you can navigate the energies of Venus square Uranus with a sense of adventure and personal growth.

21 Sunday

Sun opposed Saturn's astrological aspect, which can bring a sense of self-doubt or a feeling of being weighed down by responsibilities. However, with the New Moon and the Moon's ingress into Libra, there is an opportunity for a fresh start and a chance to find balance and harmony in your emotional and personal life. The New Moon marks a time of new beginnings, making it an ideal moment to set intentions and focus on what you want to achieve in the coming lunar cycle.

22 Monday

As Mars moves into Scorpio, you may feel a shift in your energy and approach to tackling challenges. This astrological influence enhances your determination and intensity, making you more focused on pursuing goals. The September Equinox creates a sense of equilibrium as day and night become equal. It is a time to find harmony within yourself and align with the changing seasons. As the Sun enters Libra, you may desire unity and cooperation in your relationships.

23 Tuesday

Sun opposed Neptune. Embrace this period as an opportunity for reflection and inner exploration, but be mindful of the need to differentiate between fantasy and reality. Seek clarity and discernment, and use this time to connect with your intuition and inner wisdom, allowing you to navigate through the foggy influences of the Sun-Neptune opposition with a greater sense of self-awareness and authenticity.

24 Wednesday

With the Sun forming trines to Uranus and Pluto, you may experience powerful transformation and breakthroughs. This astrological alignment enhances your sense of individuality and empowers you to embrace change. The trine to Uranus sparks a desire for freedom and innovative thinking, encouraging you to explore new horizons and express your unique self. Meanwhile, the trine to Pluto brings deep inner strength and the potential for significant personal growth.

25 Thursday

You can ignite a cosmic burst of productivity as the celestial energies align to propel you toward your professional goals. Let the stars be your guiding light in navigating tasks and deadlines, infusing your workdays with a sense of accomplishment and efficiency. This period invites you to harness the cosmic forces to optimize your productivity and set the stage for success. Dancing with the cosmic rhythm of adaptability offers an opportunity for growth and evolution.

26 Friday

As the Moon moves into Sagittarius, you may feel a sense of adventure and optimism. This astrological shift enhances your desire for exploration and a broader world understanding. You might crave intellectual stimulation and new experiences that expand your horizons. The Sagittarius Moon encourages you to embrace spontaneity and follow your curiosity, making it an ideal time to embark on a journey of self-discovery.

27 Saturday

The celestial canvas paints strokes of inspiration, igniting a surge of creative energy in your life. Whether you're an artist, writer, or simply exploring a new hobby, embrace the cosmic sparks that fuel your imagination. This auspicious time beckons you to engage in creative endeavors, allowing your unique expressions to flourish. Unleash the artist within, explore uncharted creative territories, and let the joy of self-expression be your guiding light.

28 Sunday

Under the cosmic gaze, your home takes center stage, inviting a theme of improvement and transformation. Consider this celestial encouragement as an opportunity to make positive changes within your living space. Whether it's decluttering to create a serene environment, redecorating to infuse new energy, or organizing to enhance functionality, each action contributes to the creation of a more harmonious and pleasant home sanctuary.

OCTOBER

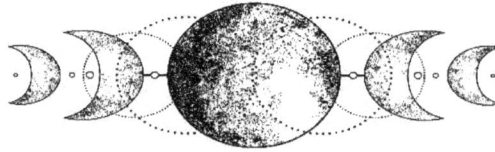

MOON MAGIC

Sun	Mon	Tue	Wed	Thu	Fri	Sat
			1	2	3	4
5	6	7	8	9	10	11
12	13	14	15	16	17	18
19	20	21	22	23	24	25
26	27	28	29	30	31	

NEW MOON

HUNTERS MOON

29 Monday

As the Moon enters Capricorn, you may notice a shift towards a more practical and disciplined emotional state. Capricorn's influence encourages you to focus on your long-term goals and responsibilities, fostering a sense of determination and self-discipline. During this lunar transition, you might feel a more substantial need for structure and organization in your daily life. Emotions may become more reserved and focused on achieving tangible results.

30 Tuesday

In the expansive ninth house, your Libra Sun infuses your quest for knowledge and philosophy with a sense of harmony and fairness. You approach life with a diplomatic and open-minded perspective, seeking to understand diverse cultures and viewpoints. Your natural ability to find common ground makes you a bridge between different ideologies. Be cautious of indecision and strive to develop a more assertive approach when it comes to pursuing your beliefs and ideals.

1 Wednesday

As the Moon enters Aquarius, you may experience a heightened sense of individuality and a desire for intellectual exploration. This astrological influence encourages you to embrace uniqueness and think outside the box. Aquarius' energy fosters a love for innovative ideas and a willingness to engage in conversations that challenge conventional thinking. However, with Mercury square Jupiter, there is a potential for information overload or exaggeration.

2 Thursday

In the tenth house, Mars in Scorpio influences your approach to career, public image, and authority with intensity, strategic thinking, and a desire for transformation. Your assertiveness is expressed through a determined pursuit of professional goals, often involving roles that require investigative skills or leadership in crises. You may find fulfillment in career paths related to psychology, research, or areas that allow you to uncover hidden truths.

3 Friday

Touching base with friends helps you discover a more connected social network. It triggers a path that nurtures well-being and harmony. Life becomes more balanced as you lay the groundwork for a stable and secure networking environment. Deepening friendships stimulates your mind and encourages an optimistic outlook. It has you feeling lighter and ready to enjoy a more supportive environment.

4 Saturday

As the Moon moves into Pisces, you may immerse yourself in a world of emotions and imagination. You could experience vivid dreams or heightened psychic experiences during this lunar transit. Embrace the Pisces Moon's energy to tap into your emotional depth and explore the realms of spirituality and compassion. Allow your emotions to flow and trust your intuition, as this can lead to profound insights and a deeper understanding of yourself and the world around you.

5 Sunday

In the transformative eighth house, Venus in Virgo indicates a deep and analytical approach to matters of shared resources, intimacy, and regeneration. Your energy is directed toward creating stability and order in shared finances, and you may find fulfillment in cultivating deep emotional connections with a focus on practical expressions of love. Balance your desire for order with the emotional depth required for transformative experiences in your relationships.

6 Monday

With the Moon moving into Aries, you may experience dynamic and assertive energy. This astrological influence encourages you to take initiative and approach situations with confidence. Your emotions become fiery and bold, urging you to embrace challenges. However, as Mercury enters Scorpio, your thinking becomes more profound and intense. The combined energies of the Aries Moon and Mercury in Scorpio offer the transformative potential of profound insights.

7 Tuesday

Full Moon. Mercury square Pluto. During a Full Moon, you might experience heightened emotions and a sense of culmination. This astrological phase brings illumination and a spotlight on specific areas of your life, revealing what is hiding. With Mercury square Pluto, there's a potential for intense thoughts and deep, probing conversations. This aspect can lead to a desire to uncover hidden truths beneath the surface.

8 Wednesday

As the Moon moves into Taurus, you might experience a sense of comfort and stability settling over your emotions. This astrological shift encourages you to indulge in the pleasures of life. With Venus forming a sextile to Jupiter, harmonious energy enhances your relationships and social interactions. Embrace the Taurus Moon's power to create a soothing and nurturing atmosphere around you, and use the Venus-Jupiter sextile's energy to embrace your connections.

9 Thursday

Your career trajectory is intricately written in the celestial scrolls, promising a chapter illuminated by growth and prosperity. As you step into this optimistic phase, the cosmos invites you to deepen your knowledge and refine your skills. Envision yourself as a cosmic scholar, exploring the infinite realms of learning that the stars unveil. Let the cosmic energies guide you toward professional excellence and success with unwavering optimism.

10 Friday

As the Moon enters Gemini, you may feel a shift towards mental curiosity and increased communication. This astrological influence encourages you to engage your mind in various discussions and seek out new sources of information. Gemini's energy fosters adaptability and a desire to connect with others through lively conversations. You might be more inclined to multitask during this lunar transit and explore different interests.

11 Saturday

Venus opposed Saturn's astrological aspect, which can bring a sense of distance or coldness in your interactions with others. It's essential to be aware of any feelings of isolation or self-doubt that may arise. While this opposition can temporarily dampen your sense of connection and affection, it also offers growth and introspection opportunities. It's a time to reevaluate your values and commitments and confront any insecurities affecting your relationships.

12 Sunday

As the Moon moves into Cancer, you may notice a shift towards heightened emotional sensitivity and a desire for comfort and security. This astrological influence encourages you to connect with your feelings deeper and seek solace in familiar and nurturing environments. Cancer's energy fosters a sense of empathy and compassion, making it an excellent time to connect with loved ones and offer support.

13 Monday

As Venus moves into Libra, you may experience a shift towards a greater emphasis on harmony, balance, and relationships. This astrological transition encourages you to seek fairness and cooperation in your interactions with others. Libra's energy fosters a desire for companionship and a deep appreciation for beauty and aesthetics. During this period, you might be drawn to social gatherings, artistic pursuits, and activities promoting a sense of connection.

14 Tuesday

Venus opposed Neptune's astrological aspect, which can bring a sense of uncertainty and illusions in your relationships and desires. However, with Pluto turning direct, there's potential for transformation and empowerment. As the Moon moves into Leo, your emotions become expressive and vibrant, encouraging you to seek creative self-expression. Venus forming trines to Uranus and Pluto adds excitement and intensity to your emotional landscape.

15 Wednesday

Cultivate a mid-week cosmic garden of gratitude as the stars inspire a mindful appreciation of life's blessings. Let celestial energies guide you in recognizing and expressing gratitude for the positive aspects of your daily existence. This mid-week period invites you to infuse each moment with cosmic appreciation, fostering a sense of gratitude that transcends the routine of the workweek. Your daily tasks become less grind and more blessed as you resonate optimism and joy.

16 Thursday

Moon ingress Virgo astrological influence encourages you to focus on organization and efficiency in your tasks. Virgo's energy fosters a desire for cleanliness and order, making it an excellent time to tackle chores and responsibilities. You might find satisfaction in caring for the more minor things that contribute to your overall well-being. This lunar transit also enhances your analytical skills, allowing you to solve problems and make precise decisions.

17 Friday

When the Sun forms a square aspect to Jupiter, you may experience a surge of enthusiasm and optimism. This astrological influence can bring a sense of expansiveness and a desire for growth. While it's natural to feel motivated to take on new challenges, be cautious of overextending yourself or making grand plans without considering the practicalities. There's a potential for overconfidence or overestimating the outcomes.

18 Saturday

Navigate the celestial waters of creativity, where the cosmic energies encourage imaginative pursuits. Whether it's a spontaneous creative gathering with friends or a day devoted to artistic expression, allow the stars to be your guides. This cosmic period invites you to explore the limitless realms of creativity, creating moments filled with the magic of artistic expression and collaborative endeavors. The magic of collaborative creativity creates a masterpiece of happiness.

19 Sunday

Moon ingress Libra astrological influence encourages you to seek balance and cooperation in your interactions with others. Libra's energy fosters a sense of diplomacy and a willingness to find common ground, making it an ideal time for engaging in social activities and fostering meaningful relationships. During this lunar transit, you may find yourself more attuned to the needs and feelings of those around you, valuing fairness and understanding in your exchanges.

20 Monday

When Mercury is conjunct with Mars, you may experience heightened mental activity and assertiveness. This astrological alignment brings energy to your thoughts and communication style. Your mind becomes sharp and focused, allowing you to express your ideas with confidence and directness. Use the Mercury-Mars conjunction's energy to be proactive in your communication and take decisive action.

21 Tuesday

During a New Moon, you may experience a period of fresh beginnings. This astrological phase marks a time of planting seeds for the future and embarking on a new cycle. As the Moon moves into Scorpio, your emotions become more intense and introspective. Scorpio's energy fosters a desire for transformation and a deeper understanding of your inner world. This lunar transition encourages you to delve into your emotions and embrace change as a means of personal growth.

22 Wednesday

As Neptune moves into Pisces, you may experience a heightened intuition and a deeper connection to your spiritual self. This astrological transition fosters a greater attunement to your subconscious and the world beyond the material realm. Neptune's energy encourages you to explore your dreams, imagination, and artistic creativity. During this period, you might find yourself more compassionate and empathetic, seeking to connect with others on a soulful level.

23 Thursday

Sun ingress Scorpio As the Sun moves into Scorpio, you may experience a shift towards a more intense emotional focus. This astrological transition encourages you to explore the hidden aspects of yourself and your surroundings. Scorpio's energy fosters a desire for transformation and a willingness to confront your inner truths. During this solar transit, you might be more inclined to seek meaningful connections and engage in reflective activities.

24 Friday

Mercury trine Jupiter enhances communication and intellectual pursuits. This alignment fosters an optimistic and open-minded atmosphere, encouraging you to engage in meaningful conversations and seek opportunities for learning and growth. Use the combined energies of the Sagittarius Moon, Sun square Pluto, and Mercury trine Jupiter to navigate your experiences' depth and expansiveness, allowing for evolution and embracing positive change.

25 Saturday

When Mercury forms a trine aspect to Saturn, you may experience a period of enhanced mental discipline and practical thinking. This astrological alignment encourages you to approach your tasks and communication with a structured and systematic mindset. Your thoughts become more focused, and your attention to detail heightens. This trine brings a favorable influence on planning, organizing, and tackling more severe or complex matters.

26 Sunday

As the Moon moves into Capricorn, you might notice a shift towards a more disciplined and goal-oriented emotional state. This astrological transition encourages you to focus on your responsibilities and strive for practical achievements. Capricorn's energy fosters a sense of determination and a willingness to work hard to reach your ambitions. During this lunar transit, you might find satisfaction in adhering to a structured routine.

27 Monday

Life settles into an enriching phase that helps you gain traction on advancing your skills. Grounding yourself in the basics lets you get involved with building a sound stage of rising prospects that progresses life forward. You reveal a fresh chapter of exciting options as you refine your abilities and connect with the vibrant landscape of possibility. An idea you discover soon develops into a blossoming path forward in your life.

28 Tuesday

With Mars forming a trine to Jupiter, you may experience increased confidence and energy. This astrological alignment enhances your drive and enthusiasm, encouraging you to pursue your goals with optimism and vigor. Your actions become more expansive, and you might take calculated risks and seek growth opportunities. This trine fosters a harmonious blend of assertiveness and wisdom, allowing you to make confident decisions and take decisive actions.

29 Wednesday

With Mars trine Saturn, there's a harmonious balance between your drive and your discipline, enabling you to pursue your ambitions with methodical determination. However, the Mercury-Uranus opposition can bring unexpected twists, challenging your plans and prompting you to think outside the box. Embrace the dynamic energy of these transits to engage in intellectual exploration, harness your motivation, and navigate shifts in your perspective with adaptability.

30 Thursday

With Mercury forming a sextile to Pluto, you may experience a period of heightened mental acuity and depth in your thoughts and communication. This astrological alignment empowers you to delve into complex subjects and uncover hidden truths. Your mind becomes wiser and more capable of grasping intricate details. This sextile encourages you to engage in meaningful conversations and research that allow you to gain profound insights.

NOVEMBER

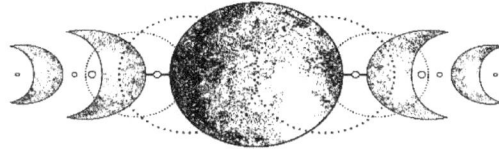

MOON MAGIC

Sun	Mon	Tue	Wed	Thu	Fri	Sat
						1
2	3	4	5	6	7	8
9	10	11	12	13	14	15
16	17	18	19	20	21	22
23	24	25	26	27	28	29
30						

New Moon

_____

_____

_____

_____

_____

_____

_____

_____

_____

_____

_____

_____

_____

_____

_____

_____

_____

_____

_____

BEAVER MOON

31 Friday

Moon ingress Pisces. During this lunar transit, you might find yourself more attuned to the subtle energies around you and drawn to artistic and imaginative activities that allow you to express your emotions. Embrace the Pisces Moon's power to nurture your emotional well-being, explore your creativity, and connect with the deeper aspects of your psyche, fostering a sense of inner peace and a greater understanding of yourself and others.

1 Saturday

The Sun in Scorpio gracing your tenth house intensifies your ambitions and career pursuits. Your determined and wise nature is channeled into achieving success through depth and transformation. You may be drawn to healing or uncovering mysteries where your ability to uncover hidden truths is a valuable asset. Be mindful of power dynamics in your professional life, and strive to use your influence ethically, recognizing the impact of your actions.

2 Sunday

With the Moon moving into Aries, you may experience a surge of energy and a desire for action. This astrological influence encourages you to be more assertive and take initiative in your emotions and pursuits. Aries' energy fosters a sense of independence and a willingness to embrace challenges head-on. However, Venus square Jupiter has the potential for overindulgence and extravagance. This aspect can create a desire for more but could lead to unrealistic expectations.

3 Monday

New options help you craft a journey that utilizes your talents to stunning effect. It brings pathways of growth that raise the potential around your life. It enables you to extend your reach into a new area worth your time. A spotlight on working with your abilities brings a pleasing result. It allows you to restore stability in what has been an uncertain time. Understanding your inherent strengths and skills helps you head towards advancement.

4 Tuesday

With Mars forming a trine to Neptune, you may experience a period of heightened creativity and a desire for inspired action. This astrological alignment empowers you to channel your energy into artistic and spiritual pursuits. As Mars moves into Sagittarius, your actions become infused with a sense of adventure and a willingness to explore new horizons. However, with the Moon moving into Taurus, you may seek comfort and stability in your emotions.

5 Wednesday

During a Full Moon, you may experience a heightened sense of culmination and emotions. This astrological phase marks completion and clarity when the Moon's illumination brings things to light. It's an opportunity to reflect on your intentions during the New Moon and evaluate your progress. The Full Moon often highlights contrasts and opposing energies, inviting you to find the balance between different areas of your life.

6 Thursday

Mars sextile Pluto astrological alignment empowers you to channel your energy towards transformative actions and focused pursuits. As the Moon moves into Gemini, your emotions become more adaptable and communicative. This lunar transition encourages you to engage in conversations and gather information from various sources. Simultaneously, with Venus moving into Scorpio, your desires may deepen, and your relationships might become more intense and passionate.

7 Friday

As Mars ignites your 11th house, your social circles and group endeavors become infused with dynamic and passionate energy. Your assertiveness within friendships and community activities is pronounced, and you take a leadership role in collaborative projects. Your friends and associates admire your drive, enthusiasm, and ability to inspire collective action. You thrive in environments that encourage growth, innovation, and shared goals.

8 Saturday

With Uranus moving into Taurus, you may enter a period of significant change and innovation in areas related to your material world and values. This astrological shift encourages you to embrace new ways of thinking about stability and resources. However, with Venus forming a square with Pluto, there's potential for intense emotions and power dynamics in relationships. This aspect can bring forth hidden tensions and a need to transform heart matters.

9 Sunday

As Mercury turns retrograde, you may experience introspection and review in your communication and thought processes. This astrological phenomenon can bring a sense of slowing down and revisiting matters from the past. It's a time to be cautious in your communication, as misunderstandings and delays could be more prevalent. This retrograde invites you to reflect on your plans, projects, and decisions, allowing you to refine your approach and address unresolved issues.

10 Monday

With the Moon moving into Leo, you may notice a shift toward a more expressive and confident emotional state. This astrological transition encourages you to embrace individuality and let your personality shine. Leo's energy fosters a desire for attention and recognition, prompting you to seek out experiences that bring you joy and allow you to showcase your creativity. You draw lively activities and engage in social interactions during this lunar transit.

11 Tuesday

Jupiter turns retrograde. It's a time to reflect on your goals, aspirations, and how you've been expanding your horizons. This period offers a chance to delve deeper into your philosophies and seek a greater understanding of your life's purpose. Embrace Jupiter's retrograde energy as an invitation to look within, reevaluate your path, and make any necessary adjustments to ensure your journey aligns with your true intentions and desires.

12 Wednesday

With Mercury conjunct with Mars, you may experience intensified mental activity and assertive communication. This astrological alignment gives you a direct and dynamic approach to expressing your thoughts and ideas. Your mind becomes sharp and decisive, allowing you to act swiftly on your plans. As the Moon moves into Virgo, your emotions become practical and detail-oriented. This combination encourages you to engage in tasks that require precision and organization.

13 Thursday

With Venus gracing your tenth house, a sense of charm and diplomacy infuses your professional life and public image. Your approach to career becomes marked by grace, creativity, and a desire for harmonious relationships in the workplace. You may find joy in roles that involve aesthetics, diplomacy, or artistic expression. Your interactions with authority figures are likely to be positive, and you may use your social skills to advance your professional goals.

14 Friday

New options ahead hold a refreshing change. It brings a buzz of activity around your social life, catching up with friends. Change is swirling around your social life; meeting new people draws companionship and support. Your social life heats up with new possibilities and invitations to go out with your friends. Sharing with others solidifies the foundations of your life and helps build a happy path forward. It generates a time of lively opportunities to entertain with friends.

15 Saturday

Moon ingress Libra. During this lunar transition, you might find yourself drawn to social activities and engaging in conversations that create understanding and unity. Your sense of aesthetics may inspire you to appreciate beauty in your surroundings and perhaps engage in creative pursuits. Embrace the Libra Moon's energy to foster meaningful connections, create an atmosphere of grace, and seek out the shared values that bring people together in a spirit of mutual respect.

16 Sunday

In the cosmic stillness, take a moment for personal introspection and growth reflections. The planetary shifts create an environment conducive to self-discovery and contemplation. Assess your goals, values, and aspirations with a discerning eye. Consider the areas of your life where personal development beckons, and set intentions to navigate the cosmic journey towards self-realization and a more authentic version of yourself.

17 Monday

With the Sun forming trines to Jupiter and Saturn, you may experience a period of balanced expansion and grounded growth. This astrological alignment empowers you with a harmonious blend of optimism and practicality. The Sun trine Jupiter encourages you to confidently embrace opportunities, while the Sun trine Saturn adds discipline and stability to your endeavors. As Mercury forms a sextile to Pluto, your communication becomes more profound and insightful.

18 Tuesday

In the tenth house, Venus in Scorpio influences your approach to career, public image, and authority with intensity, passion, and a desire for depth in your professional pursuits. You express your creative and harmonious side through career choices that involve depth, transformation, or areas that require investigative skills. You find fulfillment in roles that allow you to uncover hidden truths or bring about positive transformation.

19 Wednesday

As Mercury moves into Scorpio, your thoughts and communication may take on a perceptive quality. This astrological transition encourages you to uncover hidden truths beneath the surface. However, with Mercury opposed to Uranus, there's a potential for sudden insights and unexpected shifts in your thinking. This aspect could bring about surprises or disruptions in your communication. Yet, the Mercury trine Neptune aspect adds intuition and creativity to your expression.

20 Thursday

The New Moon astrological phase marks the planting of seeds for future growth and setting intentions. As the Sun conjuncts Mercury, your thoughts and communication align with your sense of self. With Mercury moving into Sagittarius, your thinking becomes more expansive and open to new perspectives. The Uranus sextile Neptune aspect adds a touch of innovative inspiration, allowing you to tap into your intuition and creativity.

21 Friday

As the Sun opposes Uranus, you might experience a period of unexpected disruptions and a desire for change. This astrological aspect can bring about a sense of restlessness and a need to break free from routine. While it may introduce challenges, it can encourage you to embrace innovation and liberation. Concurrently, the Sun trine Neptune aspect adds a touch of enchantment and sensitivity to your experience.

22 Saturday

As the Sun moves into Sagittarius, you may feel a shift towards a more adventurous and optimistic energy. This astrological transition encourages you to embrace exploration and expand your horizons. With Mercury forming a trine to Saturn, your thoughts and communication become practical, making it a favorable time for efficient planning and executing tasks. As the Moon moves into Capricorn, your emotions may focus more on responsibilities and goals.

23 Sunday

Sun sextile Pluto is a favorable time to shed light on hidden aspects of your life and make positive shifts. Embrace the Sun-Pluto sextile's energy to tap into your resilience and courage, allowing you to embark on self-discovery and empowerment. Use this cosmic synergy to navigate challenges with determination and to harness the potential for positive change and personal growth. This sextile encourages you to take steps towards your goals with determination and purpose.

24 Monday

Advancing your life into unique areas takes you towards growth and rising prospects. Being adaptable and open to growing your life supports your dreams, allowing unique opportunities to crop up in your life. It leads to a richly creative and expressive environment that nurtures your well-being. It lets you channel excess energy into a journey imbued with potential and possibility. It connects you with kindred spirits who share similar values.

25 Tuesday

With Mercury forming a conjunction with Venus, you may experience harmonious and pleasant communication. This astrological alignment empowers you with a charming and diplomatic way of expressing yourself. Your interactions may become more graceful and considerate, making it a favorable time for discussions that require compromise and understanding. As the Moon moves into Aquarius, your emotions may become more detached and forward-thinking.

26 Wednesday

Venus trines Jupiter. Venus trine Saturn. This combination invites you to find a healthy balance between your pleasures and your responsibilities. Embrace the Venus-Jupiter trine's energy to enhance your relationships with optimism and generosity. Let the Venus-Saturn trine inspire you to build lasting, meaningful connections based on mutual respect and commitment. Allow this cosmic synergy to guide harmony and fulfillment in your relationships and endeavors.

27 Thursday

Thanksgiving, a time of gratitude and togetherness, takes on a dreamy and compassionate quality as the Moon moves into Pisces. This astrological transition encourages you to embrace empathy and sensitivity in your interactions with loved ones. Pisces' energy fosters a sense of unity and a willingness to connect on a deeper, more emotional level. It's an opportune moment to share heartfelt moments and express your appreciation for the people and blessings in your life.

28 Friday

Saturn's direct motion encourages you to face challenges head-on, implement practical solutions, and work diligently towards your ambitions. Embrace this shift as an opportunity to make meaningful progress in areas where you feel a sense of restriction or delay. With Saturn's guidance, you can take steady steps towards achieving your aspirations and laying a solid foundation for your future endeavors.

29 Saturday

As Mercury turns direct, you may experience a sense of relief and clarity in your communication and decision-making. This astrological event marks the end of the retrograde period, which can often bring about confusion and delays in various aspects of life. With Mercury moving forward, you'll likely find it easier to express yourself clearly, resolve misunderstandings, and make decisions more confidently.

30 Sunday

With the Moon moving into Aries, you may experience a surge of energy and a desire for independence and action. This astrological transition encourages you to assert yourself and pursue your passions with vigor. However, with Venus opposed to Uranus, there's potential for disruptions and unexpected developments in your relationships and values. This aspect can create a need for freedom and a desire to break free from routine.

December

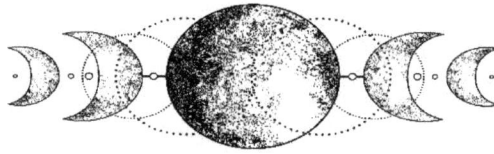

MOON MAGIC

Sun	Mon	Tue	Wed	Thu	Fri	Sat
	1	2	3	4	5	6
7	8	9	10	11	12	13
14	15	16	17	18	19	20
21	22	23	24	25	26	27
28	29	30	31			

NEW MOON

COLD MOON

1 Monday

In the tenth house, Mercury in Scorpio influences your approach to career, public image, and authority with intensity, strategic thinking, and a desire for depth in your professional pursuits. Your communication style is authoritative and passionate, and you may excel in roles that involve investigation, research, or uncovering hidden truths. Your ideas may be transformative, and you express your thoughts with conviction and depth.

2 Tuesday

With the Moon moving into Taurus, you may seek comfort, stability, and a deeper connection to the physical world. This astrological shift encourages you to indulge in life's sensual pleasures and to embrace a slower, more deliberate pace. As Venus forms a sextile to Pluto, there's an undercurrent of intensity and transformation in your relationships and desires. This aspect invites you to explore the depths of your emotional connections and to transform any unfulfilling elements.

3 Wednesday

The cosmic stage is set for a stellar performance in your professional journey, hinting at a forthcoming transformation. As you teeter on the precipice of change, a celestial waltz of growth and expansion beckons. This auspicious phase invites you to seize fresh opportunities and explore uncharted territories in your career. Let the cosmic winds guide you toward unimagined heights, where optimism and ambition intertwine, propelling you toward a radiant future.

4 Thursday

Moon ingress Gemini. The Full Moon astrological phase often brings to light matters that have been building since the New Moon, culminating in clarity and realization. It's a time when your thoughts and emotions align, encouraging you to express your feelings and ideas more openly. The Gemini influence fosters curiosity and adaptability, making it an ideal time for engaging in meaningful conversations and gathering information.

5 Friday

In the eleventh house, Mars in Sagittarius influences your approach to friendships, group activities, and societal pursuits with energy, enthusiasm, and a desire for shared exploration. You assert yourself assertively within social circles, often taking a leadership role in group activities or causes that align with your values. Your energy is directed toward creating positive change and promoting growth within your community.

6 Saturday

With the Moon moving into Cancer, you may experience heightened emotional sensitivity and a desire for comfort and security. This astrological transition encourages you to connect with your feelings and create a nurturing environment for yourself and your loved ones. Cancer's energy makes it an ideal time for cozy and heartfelt moments. Additionally, with Mercury forming a trine with Neptune, your communication takes on a more compassionate and intuitive quality.

7 Sunday

Amidst the cosmic expanse, a reflective energy invites you to delve into the realms of inner growth. Let the universal energies be your guiding light as you embark on a journey of self-discovery and personal development. This celestial dance encourages you to embrace introspection, cultivate resilience, and align your inner growth with the cosmic evolution unfolding around you. Witness the magic of abundance as it weaves through the intricate patterns of your life.

8 Monday

Amidst the expansive cosmic tableau, the theme of visionary perspectives unfolds as a celestial revelation. Seize this cosmic invitation to expand your vision for the future. Whether contemplating personal growth or envisioning the trajectory of your professional life, let the cosmic alignment broaden your horizons. It is a moment to tap into visionary insights, transcend limitations, and set your sights on the boundless possibilities that lie ahead.

9 Tuesday

Mars square Saturn's astrological aspect can bring a sense of frustration and limitations in your actions and ambitions. It's essential to be prepared for delays and setbacks during this time, as Saturn's influence tends to slow down the usually assertive energy of Mars. While it might feel like an uphill battle, this cosmic alignment also offers an opportunity to develop patience, resilience, and a more strategic approach to your goals.

10 Wednesday

With the Moon moving into Virgo, you may experience a more analytical and detail-oriented emotional state. This astrological transition encourages you to pay attention to practical matters and seek efficiency in your daily routines. Virgo's energy fosters a desire for order and a focus on self-improvement. Additionally, as Neptune turns direct, you may feel a gradual lifting of the fog that has surrounded your dreams and intuition during its retrograde phase.

11 Thursday

Mercury trine Neptune. Mercury ingress Sagittarius. This cosmic combination encourages you to communicate your beliefs and visions enthusiastically and optimistically. Embrace the Mercury-Neptune trine's energy to engage in compassionate and imaginative conversations while allowing Mercury in Sagittarius to inspire new experiences, perspectives, and opportunities for growth as you navigate this period of expanded thinking and open-mindedness.

12 Friday

With the Moon's graceful entrance into Libra, you might sense an air of harmony and a desire for balance settling into your emotional landscape. This astrological shift encourages you to seek equilibrium in your interactions with others. Libra's energy, marked by its affinity for beauty and diplomacy, invites you to appreciate the aesthetics of your surroundings and foster connections built on fairness and mutual respect.

13 Saturday

With Mercury forming a sextile to Pluto, your thoughts and communication may take on a more profound quality. This astrological alignment empowers you to explore complex subjects and engage in conversations that delve beneath the surface. It's as if a key has unlocked a door to hidden insights and transformative dialogues. This cosmic synergy encourages you to express your thoughts with intensity and precision, making it an ideal time for research or investigation.

14 Sunday

With Mars forming a square to Neptune, you might face a complex interplay between your drive and your dreams. This astrological aspect can bring a sense of ambiguity and confusion to your actions and motivations. It's as if a fog obscures your path, making it challenging to assert yourself. You may encounter situations where it's difficult to distinguish between assertive determination and impulsive escapism.

15 Monday

As Mars enters Capricorn, your energy becomes disciplined and ambitious, motivating you to pursue your goals with patience and a structured approach. It invites you to tap into your inner strength and resilience, making it an ideal period for tackling tasks that require determination and long-term planning. Embrace the Scorpio Moon's intensity to delve into matters of the heart and psyche while allowing Mars in Capricorn to guide objectives with a strategic mindset.

16 Tuesday

You can look forward to a refreshing change of pace. Prospects are heightening, bringing new terrain to explore. Indeed, several exciting avenues of growth light a path forward. It helps release the limitations that have blocked progress lately. It breaks up stagnant energy patterns and brings an energizing chapter to light. It brings a focus on social opportunities and gives you a chance to mingle with your broader circle of friends.

17 Wednesday

Sun square Saturn's astrological aspect can create a challenging dynamic where your ambitions and desires may be met with a need for extra effort and patience. It's as if you're being asked to confront limitations and work diligently to achieve goals. However, as the Moon moves into Sagittarius, you'll experience a boost of optimism and a desire for exploration. This lunar influence encourages you to seek new horizons and embrace an adventurous and open-minded perspective.

18 Thursday

In the eleventh house, Mercury in Sagittarius influences your approach to friendships, group activities, and societal pursuits with curiosity, optimism, and a desire for shared exploration. Your communication within social circles is open-minded and freedom-loving, contributing to dynamic and engaging group discussions. You may express your ideas assertively in causes related to education, philosophy, or cultural exchange.

19 Friday

Under the expansive cosmic tapestry, the focus shifts to the emotional resonances of personal connections. Feel the subtle vibrations of universal energies as you engage with loved ones and acquaintances. This celestial dance is an exploration of the heart's connections, where emotions harmonize with the cosmic frequencies, creating a tapestry of meaningful and soulful relationships. It encourages open communication, understanding, and deeper connections.

20 Saturday

With the arrival of a New Moon, you're entering a phase of fresh beginnings. This lunar event marks a time to plant seeds for the future and initiate new projects. As the Moon moves into Capricorn, you'll feel a focus on practicality, responsibility, and a desire for long-term success. Simultaneously, the Black Moon's ingress into Sagittarius adds a touch of exploration and a thirst for knowledge. It encourages you to seek higher truths and expand your horizons.

21 Sunday

With the Sun forming a square to Neptune, you may feel confusion creeping into your life. This astrological aspect can blur the lines between reality and illusion, making it challenging to make decisive choices. It's essential to be cautious about misinformation or deception during this period. Simultaneously, Venus square Saturn adds a touch of restriction and seriousness to matters of the heart and finances, potentially leading to relationship or money-related tensions.

22 Monday

As the Moon moves into Aquarius, you might sense a shift in your emotional landscape towards a more open and progressive mindset. This astrological transition encourages you to embrace your uniqueness and individuality. Aquarius' energy fosters a sense of freedom and a desire to connect with like-minded people who share your innovative ideals. You may be drawn to causes and communities that promote change and progress during this lunar transition.

23 Tuesday

The Christmas/holiday season brings a time of expansion that nurtures your life on many levels. It unlocks a chapter that transforms your world—a happy time spent sharing and collaborating with others who offer valuable guidance and ideas. It is a lovely time that draws enriching experiences and good fortune into your life. It opens the floodgates to a happier chapter that improves the potential possible in your life.

24 Wednesday

With Venus forming a square to Neptune, you might navigate a period of romantic and emotional confusion. This astrological aspect can bring about illusions and a sense of idealism in matters of the heart, making it essential to be cautious and avoid getting carried away by unrealistic fantasies or promises. Simultaneously, as Venus moves into Capricorn, you enter a phase marked by a more grounded and disciplined approach to your relationships and values.

25 Thursday

On Christmas Day, as the Moon gracefully moves into Pisces, you might sense a deepening of emotions and a desire for a more compassionate and spiritual experience. This astrological transition encourages you to embrace the essence of the holiday season, marked by love, empathy, and a sense of unity with others. Pisces' energy fosters a connection to the mystical and the ethereal, making it a perfect time to reflect on the deeper meanings of this special day.

26 Friday

Inspiring news comes out of the blue. It is a welcome remedy as an invitation to mingle brings a big plus to your social life. It offers a more socially connected phase that nurtures well-being and happiness. Sharing ideas and fascinating conversations with kindred spirits provides ample time to increase your life's stability. It lets you cross the threshold and enter a lighter and happier landscape of possibility.

27 Saturday

Moon ingress Aries astrological shift encourages you to take initiative, be more independent, and enthusiastically pursue your desires. Aries' energy is bold and adventurous, making it an ideal time to start projects, set goals, or tackle challenges head-on. You may feel spontaneous and ready to embrace opportunities for action. Use this cosmic influence to channel your inner fire and let passion shine as you navigate with self-assuredness and determination.

28 Sunday

In the reflective twelfth house, the Sun in Capricorn indicates a private and disciplined approach to spirituality, hidden knowledge, and the subconscious. Your inner self is marked by a sense of responsibility and a desire for self-mastery. You may find fulfillment in solitary pursuits that involve self-reflection, spiritual practices, or working behind the scenes. Strive to embrace moments of self-discovery and self-acceptance in your spiritual and subconscious explorations.

29 Monday

As the Moon gracefully moves into Taurus, you might notice a more grounded and steady emotional state. This astrological transition encourages you to seek comfort and security in your surroundings and to connect with the physical world. Taurus' energy fosters a desire for stability, sensuality, and a deeper connection to life's simple pleasures. During this time, you may find solace in nature, indulge in delicious meals, or seek experiences that engage your senses.

30 Tuesday

When Mercury squares Saturn, it can feel like your thoughts and communication are met with obstacles. You may encounter challenges in expressing yourself effectively, as Saturn's influence tends to bring restriction and seriousness to your mental processes. This aspect can lead to self-doubt and a tendency to overanalyze every word you say or write. Work on building confidence in your communication abilities and finding constructive ways to navigate this aspect's hurdles.

31 Wednesday

On New Year's Eve, when the Moon enters Gemini, you may feel a surge of social energy and a desire for lively interactions. This lunar placement can make you more communicative and adaptable, eager to converse with various people. You might find yourself drawn to fun and intellectually stimulating activities, such as engaging in witty conversations, playing games, or attending gatherings where you can connect with friends and acquaintances.

1 Thursday

On New Year's Day, with Mercury square Neptune and Mercury ingressing into Capricorn, you might encounter some challenges in your thinking and communication as you start the year. This cosmic alignment can cloud your thoughts and lead to misunderstandings or confusion in your conversations. It's essential to be cautious about miscommunications and double-check important messages or plans.

Astrology, Tarot & Horoscope Books.

Mystic Cat